MY objec[illegible] assemble, in concise form and simple language, various facts concerning the Church of England.

It is intended to be a guide for those hitherto ignorant of, or having forgotten, the information which it contains, and if it helps to stimulate interest in its subject it will have achieved its aim.

The Church of England is a great national heritage, but it seems to be in danger of being regarded rather as an antique curiosity than as a present-day reality. Lack of knowledge about it may have something to do with this and, therefore, I am hopeful that the contents of this book may be of use in helping to meet this deficiency.

For kindly allowing me to include copyright material my thanks are due to the following: Cambridge University Press for extracts from Bishop Hensley Henson's book *The Church of England*; Messrs. Hodder & Stoughton for a quotation from Archbishop Garbett's *In an Age of Revolution*; Oxford University Press for extracts fromArchdeacon Mayfield's *The Church of England, its Members and Business*; S.P.C.K. for extracts from *Doctrine in the Church of England*; and Canon Roger Lloyd for a quotation from the first volume of his book *The Church of England in the Twentieth Century*, published by Messrs. Longmans.

I should also like to thank my friend, Canon A. MacLeod Murray, for his help in this as in so many other matters.

F. B. C.

PREFACE

MY object in compiling this book has been to assemble, in concise form and simple language, various facts concerning the Church of England.

E. H. C.

LIST OF CONTENTS

WHAT'S WHAT

WHAT'S WHAT

A Complete Guide to the Church of England

By

F. B. CHANCELLOR

LONDON

A. R. MOWBRAY & Co. LIMITED

First published in 1960
New edition, revised 1962

PRINTED IN GREAT BRITAIN BY
A. R. MOWBRAY & CO. LIMITED IN THE CITY OF OXFORD
2429

INTRODUCTION

THE CHURCH OF ENGLAND

THE Church of England is part of the Holy, Catholic and Apostolic Church, and its members state this as their belief in the Apostles' and Nicene Creeds—Holy, as being a body set apart for God and owing its existence to His will; Catholic, as maintaining the faith of the Creeds and the Oecumenical Councils, the sacraments ordained by Christ Himself, and also the episcopate in historical succession from the apostles; Apostolic, as being linked to the early Church through an essential identity of doctrine and continuity of order.

It is of interest to note that the word Protestant does not occur either in the Creeds or in the Book of Common Prayer, and yet many who say the Creeds would assert that they are Protestants and not Catholics! The reason is, presumably, because this word 'Catholic' suggests the Church of Rome to them, while the word 'Protestant' suggests protestation against that Church, or rather its Papal authority.

It was the breaking away from the Papacy culminating in the Reformation during the reign of Henry VIII which introduced the word Protestant, and in this sense the Church may well call itself Protestant to-day. But its Catholicity far transcends its Protestantism and as part of the Catholic (in the sense of 'Universal') Church it rightly entitles itself so.

Notwithstanding, there are still divisions among Church members, and those who claim to be in possession of a historical and continuous tradition of faith and practice use the phrase Anglo-Catholic to describe themselves, while those who tend to find their ultimate standards in the Bible as interpreted on the principle of the Reformation and the sixteenth century describe themselves as Protestants.

The lack of uniformity is differently regarded, some seeing in it weakness, others a sign of strength. Yet to anyone unversed in this variety the results are often baffling.

Take, for example, two churches only a few hundred yards apart from each other in the same town, and consider what the effect upon a stranger may well be. One church is highly decorated with murals depicting the Stations of the Cross and various Saints, an altar on which there are six candlesticks, a canopied statue of the Virgin Mary with candles on either side of it, a crucifix above the pulpit, a side chapel in which the Holy Sacrament is reserved, many stained glass windows, and a faint aroma of incense permeating the whole fabric. The other is austerely plain. On the altar are two candlesticks, and there are no others, the windows are of clear glass, there are no statues, no reserved Sacrament, no crucifix, while the atmosphere is devoid of the smell of incense.

Their notice boards disclose the following facts regarding the Services which these two churches provide.

Church A

Sundays—
- Holy Communion 8.0 a.m.
- Solemn Sung Eucharist and Sermon 10.15 a.m.
- Children's Church 11.40 a.m.
- Solemn Evensong and Sermon 6.30 p.m.

Daily—Holy Communion 7.15 a.m. or 8.0 a.m.
Evensong 5.30 p.m.

Thursdays—Holy Communion 10.30 a.m.

Holy Days—Holy Communion 10.30 a.m.

Fridays—Litany and Intercessions 12.0 p.m.

Church B

Sundays—
- Holy Communion 8.0 a.m.; 12.0 on 1st and 3rd Sundays; 7.30 p.m. on 2nd Sunday in every month.
- Sunday Morning Service 11.0 a.m.
- Evensong 6.30 p.m.
- Sunday School (Parish Hall) 9.45 a.m.

Thursdays—Holy Communion 8.0 a.m.

Saints' Days—Holy Communion 8.30 a.m. and 11.30 a.m.

It will be seen how much they vary. Nor would it be difficult to find two other churches differing considerably more. The two selected are by no means as extreme in either direction as are many others. But one will appeal to the Anglo-Catholic, the other to the Protestant. Yet both belong to the Church of England, and those who worship in one or the other (whether clergy or laity) are equally members of that Church. The reason for this apparent and, indeed, very real difference in outlook is perhaps due to that spirit of compromise which, as the late Dean Inge once wrote:

> . . . has guided the Church of England at all times. It has aimed at being the nation on its spiritual side, and has not thought it necessary to be more logical or consistent than the people as a whole. For this reason, it has been abused like any other English institution. It has been, on the whole, Conservative or at least anti-revolutionary; in time of national danger it is always vehemently patriotic; but it allows the utmost latitude of divergence in all questions upon which good citizens are divided. It has kept the *via media* between 'the meretricious gaudiness of the Church of Rome, and the squalid sluttery of fanatical conventicles,' to quote a seventeenth-century divine.

There are those who deplore what they regard as the lack of discipline among the Church of England clergy. Bishop Hensley Henson was a vociferous example. But it must be remembered that all have been episcopally ordained, all celebrate the Communion, for all of them the Book of Common Prayer is the only official service book, however much they may deviate from it in certain details. And it must also be remembered that throughout the whole range of the Church's forms of worship the emphasis lies rather on 'you may' or 'you should' than on 'you must.' There is thus a degree of freedom greater than exists in other churches both for clergy and laity.

'There is in the Church of England,' as the Chairman's introduction to the report on Doctrine in the Church of England states, 'a rich treasury of spiritual experience, a living tradition of personal devotion and freely moving thought. The same is true of every one of the schools of thought within it.'

* * *

The Church of England is both a national institution and a spiritual society, but in the latter capacity its appeal to the large mass of the people of Great Britain is not so great as it should be, or as one might hope.

There are many reasons for this state of affairs. Modern science (popularly understood) and Biblical criticism are among them. The effect of two major wars in which the country has been heavily and grievously although victoriously involved, instead of initiating a religious revival, as some hoped, has had an opposite effect. Communism must also be reckoned as a factor in the decline.

Nevertheless, in spite of the increase in the number of virtual agnostics and of a few declared atheists there is, except on the part of the Communists, who are in any case a small minority, very little actual hostility to the Church. More general is an attitude of apparent indifference.

At the same time, a rather odd sort of sense of tradition and of social behaviour still tends to make the average man and woman wish for their children to be baptized, their own marriages to be solemnized by the Church, and the Order of Burial to be read at their funerals;

but apart from these occasions they leave the Church severely alone!

It is the fashion to regard religion as an entirely personal matter ('What a man does with his own solitariness' as Professor A. N. Whitehead has suggested), and to see no need for a Christian community meeting in worship.

A recent book[1] based on the results of mass inquiry reveals some startling facts:

'Church of England—only to distinguish myself from Roman Catholic or other denomination,' is a typical answer to the inquiry of what a man's religion is. 'Christian—but not belonging to any church' is another. As to church attendance, the author estimates that only 9 per cent go regularly once a week, but rather surprisingly 6 per cent attend services more than once a week.

If the figures are correct (and statistics are liable, as everyone knows, to be unreliable), there is a small section of devoted and earnest churchmen and churchwomen in the country, but however much they may try, by example and other means, to evangelize at least some of the remainder their efforts apparently fall on stony ground.

In a materialistic society, such as ours, it is not really surprising that the Gospel of Christ does not appeal to the average man and woman. Nor, indeed, has it ever done so as a practical way of life, however much it may have been appreciated in theory. But whether owing to superstitious fear of the wrath of God descending upon them in the event of their not worshipping Him, or whether due to dislike of departing from general custom, there is no doubt that the churches as a whole formerly contained very much larger congregations than they do to-day in spite of the then far smaller population.

The prevailing popular attitude towards the person of Jesus Christ is that He was a very good man Who led a very good life; a gentle, rather effeminate figure to appeal

[1] *Exploring English Character*, by Geoffrey Gorer (1955).

maybe to children and old women, but not to men. The Christian ethic, as summed up in the second of the two great Commandments, is subscribed to in theory, and 'good neighbourliness' is regarded as the proper conduct, at any rate for one's neighbour, to adopt! Yet the first of the great Commandments is ignored, and, if it be suggested that the second is contingent on the first, the suggestion will either be scorned or not understood!

Adverse criticism is often made of both the clergy and those of the laity who form the section of regular church-goers. They are accused of being no better than anyone else and are often called hypocrites, humbugs, psalm-singers, and so on. Religion is something apart from everyday life, and those who practise it are held to be old-fashioned, cranks, people pretending to be superior to others.

The Church's attitude towards divorce and the re-marriage of divorced persons, towards birth control, towards betting and gambling, towards the use of money, towards sexual aberrations, towards war and the use of atomic weapons is unpopular.

And yet there remains among a great mass of those who think on these lines a curious streak of belief in the Christian religion. A streak which causes them to pray in times of great stress, to sing hymns (e.g. 'Abide with me') at communal gatherings such as important football matches, to regard the parish church, especially in rural districts, if not as a place in which to worship, certainly as a symbol of something they value and honour. One ventures to suggest that if the churches were closed the outcry would be nearly as great on the part of those who seldom enter one as it would be on the part of regular church-goers.

The position is a serious one for the Church whose mission is to 'present Christ Jesus in the power of the Holy Spirit, that men shall come to put their trust in God through Him, to accept Him as their Saviour, and to serve Him as their King in the fellowship of His Church.'[1]

How is it to find a substitute for the empty pews which were formerly filled by those who were thus accessible to Christian teaching? One way which is surely bound to fail is for the Church to try to compete with the entertainment business by introducing into its services all sorts of spectacular accessories.

In what, then, lies the remedy? Is it not for the faithful to be witnesses, through their own godly living, of what belief in the religion of Christ really means, in contrast with the secularity of society in general? Might not such a body tend in time to demonstrate the true values of Christian faith and win the allegiance of many who, through ignorance and indifference, at present remain aloof?

That was the way of Jesus Christ, and that is the mission of His Church.

[1] *Archbishops' Committee on the Evangelistic Work of the Church* (1918).

WHAT'S WHAT

CHAPTER ONE

THE CHURCH OF ENGLAND IN GENERAL

1. *Administration*

THE whole of England is divided into dioceses, each governed by a Bishop, and these in turn are subdivided into parishes in charge of a Rector, Vicar, or Perpetual Curate, so that there is literally no part of the country without a pastor provided by the Church.

At one time each parish had its own parish priest, but to-day, on account of the shortage of clergy and the increase in population in the towns this is impossible, and so in many instances parishes are united or held in plurality, and sometimes as many as three small parishes may have only one priest to minister to them.

On the other hand, when a parish increases very much in size, it is often divided into two with a daughter-church administered by the parish church until such time as the new district is able to support its own priest.

Groups of parishes, conveniently situated, are formed into a rural deanery under a rural dean who is usually the rector, or vicar, of one of the parishes in it. There are also a few places of worship which do not come under the jurisdiction of a Diocesan Bishop, such as the Chapels Royal, but they need not concern us here.

THE DIOCESES

They are grouped into the two Provinces of Canterbury and York, each under the jurisdiction of an Archbishop, and there are forty-three of them, as follows: Canterbury, York, London, Durham, Winchester, Bath and Wells,

Birmingham, Blackburn, Bradford, Bristol, Carlisle, Chelmsford, Chester, Chichester, Coventry, Derby, Ely, Exeter, Gloucester, Guildford, Hereford, Leicester, Lichfield, Lincoln, Liverpool, Manchester, Newcastle, Norwich, Oxford, Peterborough, Portsmouth, Ripon, Rochester, St. Albans, St. Edmundsbury and Ipswich, Salisbury, Sheffield, Sodor and Man, Southwark, Southwell, Truro, Wakefield, and Worcester. Of these, the following are in the Province of York: York, Durham, Blackburn, Bradford, Carlisle, Chester, Liverpool, Manchester, Newcastle, Ripon, Sheffield, Sodor and Man, Southwell, and Wakefield.

Except for five of these dioceses, they have been listed in alphabetical order. The reason for these exceptions is because Canterbury and York take precedence, as Archbishoprics, while London, Durham and Winchester have special significance in that the Bishops have a seat in the House of Lords, irrespective of their seniority, and their dioceses have, therefore, a superiority to those of all others in the two provinces.

Bishops sign themselves with the name of their diocese preceded by their Christian name, e.g. the Bishop of Manchester signs 'William Manchester.' In certain cases the old diocesan names are used, as follows:

Canterbury	= Cantuar	Norwich	= Norvic
York	= Ebor	Oxford	= Oxon
London	= Londin	Peterborough	= Petriburg
Winchester	= Winton	Rochester	= Roffen
Bath and Wells	= Bath : et Well :	Salisbury	= Sarum
		Truro	= Truron
Chichester	= Cicestr	Durham	= Dunelm
Exeter	= Exon	Carlisle	= Carliol
Gloucester	= Gloucestr	Chester	= Cestr

The formations of the various dioceses date from as far back as A.D. 314 (London) to as recently as 1927 (Derby, Guildford, Leicester, and Portsmouth). At one time the area covered by some of them was very considerably greater than it is to-day; e.g. Lincoln, which was the largest and extended from the Humber to the Thames, embracing the present dioceses of Oxford, Leicester and Peterborough, as well as the present Lincoln. Only Chichester retains its pre-Norman boundaries.

Sometimes the word 'see' is used to indicate a diocese, but technically it means the official seat, or throne, of a bishop, which is usually placed in the cathedral of the diocese.

Parishes

Within each diocese there are, as already stated, a number of parishes each under the spiritual care of a priest who is also known as the incumbent.

The establishment of the parochial system in England dates from the seventh century, and may have its roots in pagan times. There is no sort of uniformity with regard to size, some being large, others small. By the New Parishes Measure of 1943 the creation of new parishes is brought about by an Order in Council confirming a scheme drawn up by the Church Commissioners, who are actuated by three considerations, viz.: (i) that the spiritual interest of the area will be best served by the creation of a new parish; (ii) that a suitable church already exists or is intended to be provided; and (iii) that a suitable endowment has been or will be provided.

In practice such new parishes are confined to new towns or to existing towns and cities which have considerably increased in size. In country districts such changes as are from time to time made consist in amalgamating two or more existing parishes and the Pastoral Reorganization Measure of 1949 was designed to achieve this end which is undertaken by each Diocesan Pastoral Committee whose suggestions are submitted to the Church Commissioners.

Plurality

The holding of more than one benefice by one person at the same time is called plurality, and the benefices are said to be 'held in plurality.' Each parish retains its separate identity with its own parochial church council, churchwardens, etc. It is a temporary measure, coming to an end when the incumbent vacates the benefices, after which the parishes may return to their former independence of each other.

Union

The union of parishes under one incumbent is regarded as a permanent arrangement. The parishes concerned may either remain distinct, with their own church councils, churchwardens, etc., or they may become one with a single boundary, one church council, one set of churchwardens, etc. In the latter case both churches are used, but one becomes the parish church and the other a chapel of ease.

Parochial Church Councils

Each parish has its Parochial Church Council, usually referred to as the 'P.C.C.' These Councils are elected annually except for certain *ex officio* members who are the Minister of the parish, all licensed assistant Curates of the parish, the churchwardens, and lay members of any ruri-decanal or diocesan conference or of the Church Assembly.

Elected members must be 'Actual Communicant Members of the Church of England of twenty-one years and upwards.' The number varies according to the custom of the parish concerned, and if the Council so decides a limited number of co-opted members may be included. The duties of parochial church council members are officially summed up as being 'to co-operate with the Incumbent in the initiation, conduct and development of Church work both within the Parish and outside.' In practice a variety of subjects come up for discussion at meetings, financial matters usually occupying a considerable amount of time. The Council should meet at least four times a year.

For those who desire more detailed information the Parochial Church Councils (Powers) Measure[1] of 1956 should be consulted.

Parochial Church Meeting and Vestry

This is an annual affair which should be held in each parish not later in the year than the week following Easter Week and which all persons whose names are entered upon the roll of the parish are entitled to attend.

Various items of business such as the annual report on the proceedings of the Council and on the financial affairs of the parish are presented and can be discussed. For full information see the Representation of the Laity Measure (1956).

Sequestration

In the event of a vacancy in a benefice occurring, a Writ of Sequestration is issued by the Diocesan Bishop, who appoints Sequestrators, usually (but not invariably) the Churchwardens, and sometimes the Rural Dean also. Under the Writ the income of the benefice is ordered to be taken by the Sequestrators and to be applied by them as the circumstances of the case may require. They (the Sequestrators) pay all legally chargeable outgoings, as well as the cost of serving the parish during the vacancy, and eventually account to the new incumbent and pay him any balance which they have in hand, or, alternatively, receive from him any sum which they have properly paid in excess of what they have received.

By the Benefices (Sequestrations) Measure of 1933, the

[1] For further information regarding this and other legal matters referred to, see *A Handbook for Churchwardens and Parochial Church Councillors*, by K. Macmorran, Mowbrays, 5*s*.

Bishop has the power of fixing the amount of remuneration to be paid to clergymen undertaking occasional duty. Under this measure, too, subject to the Bishop's approval, the Sequestrators may provide out of the income of the benefice for the care and custody of the residence and the upkeep of its garden and may overdraw their banking account.

The Convocations of Canterbury and York

These are exclusively clerical assemblies and consist of an Upper and a Lower House. The Upper is composed of all the Diocesan Bishops in the Province and is presided over by the Archbishop; the Lower is composed of a number of *ex officio* members, together with others who are selected representatives of the clergy.

They meet for the inside of a week on two or three occasions during the year, each day's meeting being known as a 'session.'

The Church Assembly

This is officially designated as 'The National Assembly of the Church of England' and comprises the Upper and Lower Houses of the Convocations of Canterbury and York, together with a House of Laity. The House of Laity consists of representatives of the laity of the Provinces of Canterbury and York elected every five years by the lay members of the Diocesan Conferences, with not more than ten co-opted members.

Their deliberations cover all matters concerning the Church of England and the Chairman is the Archbishop of Canterbury, or, in his absence, the Archbishop of York or a Bishop, in order of seniority.

The Assembly is debarred from issuing pronouncements on matters of theology, which are reserved for the Convocations. Its most important function is to prepare ecclesiastical measures for transmission to Parliament. Normally it meets three times a year in London.

Diocesan and Ruri-decanal Conferences

Each Diocese and each Rural Deanery within the Diocese holds annually one or more conferences at which those members elected as representatives meet to discuss matters connected with Church Administration within their particular jurisdiction.

The Diocesan Bishop usually presides over the Diocesan Conference, and the Rural Dean over the Ruri-decanal Conference.

Within each Diocese there are various Committees, such as the Board of Finance, the Training for the Ministry Committee, the Maintenance of the Ministry Committee, the Dilapidations Board, the Religious Education Committee, the Pastoral Committee, and others which deal with their particular subjects so far as they concern the Diocese. Members of these various Committees are elected by the members of the Diocesan Conference, but the Bishop usually has authority to nominate certain additional members.

Cathedral Chapters

Each Cathedral is governed by a body of clergy consisting of from three to six residentiary Canons presided over by a Dean or Provost, who concern themselves with services, the upkeep of the building, the appointment of an organist and so on. Cathedrals and their closes (i.e. the precincts of the Cathedral) do not come within the jurisdiction of any parish.

Church Commissioners

This body was formed in 1948 by an Amalgamation of the Ecclesiastical Commissioners and Queen Anne's Bounty. Its business is to manage the estates and revenues of the Church of England and its Constitution is as follows:

The two Archbishops.
The forty-one Diocesan Bishops.
Five Deans, ten other Clerks in Holy Orders, and ten laymen appointed by the Church Assembly.
Four laymen nominated by the Crown.
Four persons nominated by the Archbishop of Canterbury.
The Lord Chancellor.
The Lord President of the Council.
The First Lord of the Treasury.
The Chancellor of the Exchequer.
The Secretary of State for the Home Department.
The Speaker of the House of Commons.
The Lord Chief Justice.
The Master of the Rolls.
The Attorney-General.
The Solicitor-General.
The Lord Mayor and two Aldermen of the City of London.
The Lord Mayor of York.
One representative each from the Universities of Oxford and Cambridge.
The three Church Estates Commissioners and Joint Treasurers.

The Board of Governors is formed of not more than thirty of the Commissioners and day-by-day business is carried on by a small Estates and Finance Committee, which includes the three Church Estates Commissioners.

There are also Legal, Architectural and Surveyors departments. Their headquarters are at 1 Millbank, Westminster, S.W.1.

Their assets are considerable, and for the year 1960–61 the income amounted to £15,765,157, none of which was provided by the State. But while the income is large so are the expenses—stipends of the clergy and pensions for the retired amounting to over £10,000,000.

Apart from their financial duties the Church Commissioners deal with such matters as the formation of new parishes, the union of existing ones, the alteration of parish boundaries, the demolition of churches no longer required, and the sale of the sites, the sale of redundant parsonage houses, and fixing the statutory fees chargeable for marriages, funerals and other rites.

Ecclesiastical Courts

1. *Provincial Courts*

(*a*) The Court of Arches is the Court of the Archbishop of Canterbury and is presided over by the Dean of Arches.

(*b*) The Chancery Court of York is the Court of the Archbishop of York and its official principal is called the Auditor.

They hear appeals from the Consistory Courts, but occasionally cases appear before them without a preliminary hearing.

There are also the following courts:

(*c*) The Archbishops' Court for the trial of heresy.
(*d*) The Archbishops' Court for the trial of bishops.
(*e*) A Court under the Benefices Act, 1898.
(*f*) A Court of Appeal under the Church Assembly Discipline Measure.
(*g*) A Commission under the Bishops (Retirement) Measure, 1956.

2. *Diocesan Courts*

(*a*) The Consistory Court (known in the Diocese of Canterbury as the Commissary Court). The judge of the Court in Canterbury is styled the Commissary-General, and in other dioceses the Chancellor.
(*b*) The Court under the Pluralities Act, 1838.
(*c*) The Court under the Church Disciplinc Act, 1840.
(*d*) *Four tribunals:*

(i) Two under the Church Discipline Act, 1840.
(ii) One under the Public Worship Regulation Act, 1874.
(iii) One under the Clergy Discipline Act, 1892.

(iv) One under the following Church Assembly Measures (The Incumbents (Discipline) Measure 1947; the Church Dignitaries (Retirement) Measure 1949; and the Incumbents (Discipline) and Church Dignitaries (Retirement) Amendment Measure 1953).

The Court of ultimate appeal is the Judicial Committee of the Privy Council.

Lambeth Conferences

The first Lambeth Conference was held in 1867, since when there have been eight others, of which the most recent took place in 1958. They are assemblies of the Bishops of the whole Anglican Communion who meet together at Lambeth Palace under the Presidency of the Archbishop of Canterbury. How greatly the numbers attending have increased may be gained from the fact that, whereas in 1867 there were 76, in 1958 there were over 300.

The Bishops deliberate and the fruit of their deliberations is advice. They do not enact canons, make decisions binding on the Church, or lay down definitions on points of doctrine. Their resolutions do not have any authority of a legislative, administrative or coercive nature. But by the very nature of the conferences it is clear that a body of Bishops meeting solemnly, invoking the aid of the Holy Spirit, and subsequently issuing a statement of their deliberations should, and in fact does, both guide and persuade Christian people throughout the world.

The Anglican Communion

By the Anglican Communion is meant all those Churches which are in communion with and recognize the leadership of the Archbishop of Canterbury, whether they are in the United Kingdom or abroad.

They are, apart from the Church of England: the

Church of Ireland; the Church in Wales; the Episcopal Church in Scotland; the Protestant Episcopal Church in the U.S.A.; the Church of India, Pakistan, Burma and Ceylon; the Church of the Province of South Africa; the Anglican Church of Canada; the Church of England in Australia and Tasmania; the Church of the Province of New Zealand; the Church of the Province of the West Indies; Nippon Sei Ko Kai (Japan Holy Catholic Church); the Church of the Province of West Africa; the Church of the Province of Central Africa.

There are also various missionary dioceses under the Archbishop of Canterbury's direct jurisdiction: East Africa; North Africa; Argentina and Eastern South America with the Falkland Islands; Bermuda; Borneo; Gibraltar; Korea; Madagascar; Mauritius; Area of North and Central Europe under the jurisdiction of the Bishop of London; Singapore; the Anglican Communion in Jerusalem and the Middle East; and Hong Kong.

In addition must be mentioned the Church of South India which is in limited intercommunion with the Church of England.

The three characteristics which these churches have in common are:

(*a*) they uphold and propagate the Catholic and Apostolic faith and order as they are generally set forth in the Book of Common Prayer as authorized in their several Churches;

(*b*) they are particular or national Churches, and, as such, promote within each of their territories a national expression of Christian faith, life and worship; and

(*c*) they are bound together not by a central legislative and executive authority, but by mutual loyalty sustained through the common counsel of the Bishops in conference.

The Bishops of the various Dioceses meet every ten years at the Lambeth Conference.

Archbishops of Canterbury since 1501 (only)

1501	Henry Dean (Sixty-eighth in succession from St. Augustine)	1758	Thomas Secker
		1768	Frederick Cornwallis
		1783	John Moore
1503	William Warham	1805	Charles Manners Sutton
1533	Thomas Cranmer		
1556	Cardinal Pole	1828	William Howley
1559	Matthew Parker	1848	John Bird Sumner
1576	Edmund Grindall	1862	Charles Thomas Longley
1583	John Whitgift		
1604	Richard Bancroft	1868	Archibald Campbell Tait
1610	George Abbot		
1633	William Laud	1883	Edward White Benson
1660	William Juxon	1896	Frederick Temple
1663	Gilbert Sheldon	1903	Randall Thomas Davidson
1678	William Sancroft		
1691	John Tillotson	1928	Cosmo Gordon Lang
1695	Thomas Tenison	1942	William Temple
1716	William Wake	1945	Geoffrey Francis Fisher
1737	John Potter		
1747	Thomas Herring	1961	Arthur Michael Ramsey
1757	Matthew Hutton		

2. *The Church and Finance*

The Church's Income

The two main sources of income of the Church of England are the funds administered by the Church Commissioners and gifts received from Church people.

The income of the Church Commissioners for the year 1960–61 was as follows:

	£
Stock Exchange Securities	8,773,534
Agricultural and Urban Estates ..	4,479,736
Mortgages	1,317,887
Miscellaneous receipts	1,194,000
Total Income	£15,765,157

This income was distributed as follows:

	Amount spent	*Proportion of each £*		
	£	£	*s.*	*d.*
Stipends of rectors and vicars ..	7,709,174		9	9¼
Stipends of curates	574,962			8¾
Stipends of Deans, Canons and Cathedral Servants	455,673			7
Stipends of Bishops, Suffragans and Archdeacons	404,578			6¼
Aditions to gifts by laity	419,703			6½
Pensions and provision for pensions	1,111,702		1	5
Parsonages	550,000			8¼
Church buildings in new areas ..	257,345			4
Church Schools	50,000			0¾
Other Church property	124,593			2
Beneficiaries under various trusts..	180,223			2¾
Reserves and Sinking Funds ..	400,525			6
General reserve for Capital or revenue	1,519,005		1	11
Irrecoverable Income Tax ..	310,871			4¾
Administration	696,803			10½
Capital account for reinvestment	1,000,000		1	3¼
	£15,765,157	£1	0	0

From these figures it will be seen that the greatest charge on the income is the stipends of the clergy.

The sources from which the Church Commissioners derive their income comprise ancient church endowments, the former possessions of the bishoprics and cathedral chapters, funds of particular livings of which they are trustees, and so on.

How the Clergy are Paid

The minimum stipend of an incumbent to-day is in the range of £500–£600, with a house free of dilapidations and rates. In addition there is the Easter Offering, certain

Fees, and possibly some payment for extra-parochial work. This shows an advance of £200 on pre-war stipends, but is offset by a higher cost of living.

The following example of an incumbent's income is given in *The Church of England* by Guy Mayfield (Archdeacon of Hastings).

Income

	£	s.	d.
Endowment Income			
(1) Church Commissioners (gross) ..	250	0	0
Other sources, viz. glebe ..	15	0	0
Gross endowment income	265	0	0
(2) Charges against income	92	0	0
Net endowment income	173	0	0
Non-endowment income			
(3) Church Commissioners Grants—Payable while benefice held as sole charge	100	0	0
(4) P.C.C. Contributions towards—			
stipend ..	50	0	0
dilapidations	35	0	0
rates ..	56	0	0
(5) Diocesan Augmentation Grants—Diocesan Stipends Fund	140	0	0
(6) Fees	15	10	6
(7) *Total net Benefice Income*	569	10	6
(8) Easter Offerings ..	30	5	3

Charges against Income

	£	s.	d.
Rates (including water rate) on parsonage house	56	0	0
Dilapidations: annual assessment ..	35	0	0
Charges payable on glebe—Cost of collecting rents	1	0	0
(2) Total of charges against income ..	92	0	0

For use of Diocesan Authorities

	£	s.	d.
Chaplaincies ..	50	0	0

Notes:

1. The endowment income of £250 paid by the Church Commissioners is the interest derived from capital sums held by them which principally take the form of compensation

money received for the extinguishment of tithe under the Tithe Act, 1936, proceeds of the sale of glebe, and capital sums received in respect of benefactions and bequests and grants made to meet them by the Commissioners.

2. The charges deducted from the endowment income are typical, and leave the benefice with £173 a year assured stipend for the incumbent.

3. Presumably some years ago, the Ecclesiastical Commissioners undertook to augment the benefice income permanently by £100 a year. If the benefice were to be joined in plurality or union with another and the stipend thereby increased, the Church Commissioners would review this payment.

4. During the post-war years the parochial church council, as a result of certain appeals, undertook these payments to increase the stipend; the full cost of rates and dilapidations was paid, and in addition a Scheme 'K' to augment the stipend by £100 was undertaken, in co-operation with the diocesan board of finance. The council pays £50 towards this amount.

5. The diocesan board of finance augments the living by £140, of which £50 is part of the Scheme 'K' mentioned above. But it was evidently considered that the resources of the parochial church council were already fully stretched by their contributions, totalling £131 a year. Nevertheless the benefice was still below the minimum of £550 a year net. The diocesan board of finance therefore raised the income to the minimum by an augmentation of £90 a year.

6. The fees are probably on the high side if it be assumed that the benefice is a rural one; but they are not too high for an average town parish.

7. The net benefice income, after the payment of dilapidations and rates, etc., as given in (2) is £569 10*s.* 6*d.* This is near enough to the minimum as not to matter, as fees may vary from year to year.

8. The incumbent receives in addition the Easter Offering of £30 5*s.* 3*d.* This also will vary annually.

9. The incumbent receives £50 in return for some chaplaincy duty, probably at a nearby hospital or private school. In some dioceses the sums received from such chaplaincies are reckoned as part of the net stipends, and in others they are

not so reckoned for purposes of augmentation. The present tendency is for such payments to be additional to net stipend since they not only involve extra work but also extra expense in transport. (A prospective incumbent, or the churchwardens, who may ask what the stipend of the benefice is, can receive a clear answer: the assured stipend is £569 10*s*. 6*d*. net, but to this may be added about £30 for Easter Offerings and another £50 for chaplaincy duties, making £650 in all.)[1]

Easter Offerings

It has long been the custom for a special offering to be made on Easter Day and given to the incumbent for his own use. This offering is liable to income tax, in whatever way it is raised! In recent times a custom has grown up of making a collection on Whitsunday for the benefit of assistant clergy. The Inland Revenue authorities regard such offerings in the same way as Easter Offerings.

The Stipends of Bishops

Under the Episcopal Endowments and Stipends Measure, 1943, the stipends of Bishops are now paid by the Church Commissioners, the minimum being £2,500 per annum and the maximum £7,500 (Canterbury). Both York and London receive £5,000, Durham £4,000, Winchester and Bradford £3,000, Bath and Wells £2,700, Carlisle £2,600.

Various expenses entailed by virtue of his office are also paid by the Church Commissioners and, with the exception of the residence of the Bishop of Sodor and Man, the official palaces are vested in and kept in repair by the Commissioners.

Clergy Pensions

Under the Clergy Pensions Measure of 1926 a Contributory pension scheme for those under the age of fifty-five on January 1st, 1927, was set up and provided

[1] *The Church of England*, by Guy Mayfield (1958).

a pension on retirement, at the age of 70, of £200 maximum for 40 or more years' service, and £34 minimum for 15 years' service. The clergy had to pay a contribution of 3 per cent of their net stipend towards this and the remainder was provided by the Church Assembly from diocesan quotas and by the Ecclesiastical Commissioners.

In 1954 the Church Commissioners undertook the responsibility for providing clergy pensions and the clergy were relieved of their former contributions. The pension was increased to a maximum of £300 a year.

Since then, pensions have been brought up to £364 for all those clergy not entitled to a State contributory pension and eligible for full pension.

In respect of clergy widows the Pensions Board now manages to ensure that every widow shall have at least £200 a year.

In addition, a certain amount of accommodation for retired clergy and their widows is available, but not nearly sufficient to meet to-day's needs.

Diocesan Finance

Each diocese has its Board of Finance to administer the diocesan funds and act as trustees of property.

These funds are chiefly obtained from: (1) Endowments, (2) parochial quota payments, (3) subscriptions, (4) special appeals, and (5) allocations from the Church Commissioners; and expended for: (1) training ordination candidates, (2) grants towards pensions for clergy, their widows and orphans, (3) religious education, (4) augmentation of clergy stipends, (5) grants for new churches and halls, (6) repairs to ancient churches, (7) contribution to the Church Assembly, (8) special needs, and (9) administration.

The parochial quota contributions provide the greater part of the income. These are derived from a percentage levy on the income of each parish in the diocese, usually of about 8–10 per cent, the basis of assessment being as a rule the average income of a parochial church council for the preceding three years, less certain deductions.

Among some parishioners this contribution to the diocesan fund is unpopular, it being thought that money contributed by the parish should be for the sole use of the parish!

The greatest expenditure of diocesan funds is in connection with the augmentation of clergy stipends and grants for new churches and halls.

The Diocesan Board of Finance is appointed by members of the Diocesan Conference and acts under their instructions.

Parochial Finance

The Parochial Church Councils are required to draw up an annual budget of church expenses and to administer the funds they collect accordingly.

The expenses for which they are responsible are:

1. Expenses relating to the church, e.g. heating, lighting, payment of organist, payments to the incumbent, and for the parsonage house (rates and dilapidations).
2. The upkeep of the fabric of the church.
3. The Diocesan Quota contribution.
4. Donations to charitable objects.

Their income comes from:

1. Collections at church services.
2. Subscriptions received for church expenses.
3. Any legacies or bequests.
4. Rent and proceeds of letting a church hall.
5. Sales of work, fêtes, etc.
6. Gift days.
7. Income from trust funds.

N.B.—Technically, collections are only those taken at church services other than the Holy Communion (where the alms should be disposed of by the minister and churchwardens as they think fit). In practice they are usually lumped together and form part of the P.C.C. funds.

The above items explain themselves, but it may be well to add a note about Free-will Offering schemes which have in many instances proved a more satisfactory method of raising money than the handing round of bag or plate.

In the Free-will Offering scheme, subscribers undertake to make a definite payment for each year. If made by deed of covenant for a period of not less than seven years and the subscriber pays income tax at the standard rate, the tax paid on the subscription is recoverable by the Council.

There is also the envelope scheme by which a subscriber receives a sufficient number of envelopes for each Sunday in the year and into which he puts his money whether he attends services or not.

3. *The Relations of Church and State*

What is meant when the Church of England is called the Established Church can be summed up as follows:

1. The Crown, on the advice of the Prime Minister, nominates the Bishops of the Church for appointment, appoints the Deans and many of the residentiary Canons of Cathedral Churches and the incumbents of a large number of parochial benefices of which it is the patron.

2. The Convocations of Canterbury and York are summoned, prorogued and dissolved by the Crown and cannot enter on ecclesiastical legislation without royal authority, nor may canons be drafted and become law without receiving the assent of the Sovereign in council.

3. Measures of the Church Assembly require the assent of the Sovereign in Parliament before they have the force of statute law.

4. The State recognizes the right of the Archbishop of Canterbury, as the Primate of All England, to anoint and crown the Sovereign.

5. The highest court of appeal in matters ecclesiastical is the Judicial Committee of the Privy Council.

6. The State provides Chaplains to the Forces and to various State institutions and pays them their stipends.

7. The State provides for the inclusion of twenty-six Bishops in the House of Lords, but excludes the Clergy from membership of the House of Commons.

8. The State secures the Bishops in their Sees and the beneficed Clergy in their 'livings,' and in consequence they can be removed only after trial, hearing, conviction and sentence, by a process of law recognized by the State.

9. The State requires that the Sovereign and the Lord Chancellor shall belong to the Church of England.

10. By its establishment of the Church the State proclaims that it is a Christian State.

Contrary to some misconceptions, the State does not maintain the Established Church out of the national exchequer, nor pay the stipends of the clergy (except a certain few in the service of the State), nor build, nor maintain, church buildings, nor support the evangelistic and pastoral work of the Church; does not require that anyone, save the Sovereign and the Lord Chancellor, shall belong to the Established Church; does not make deacons, ordain priests, nor consecrate bishops; does not impose any rules of its own devising upon the clergy in the exercise of their ministry, nor add to nor subtract from the Church's faith.

That this situation is not altogether satisfactory to many members of the Church was made abundantly clear during the debates on the revision of the Prayer Book.

It is a fact that the Bishops can be appointed by someone who is not even a member of the Church of England; it is a fact that the Church cannot revise its own forms of worship and obtain legal sanction for them without the consent of a body of men and women, many of whom may not be in communion with the Church of England;

it is a fact that the members of the final Court of Appeal in ecclesiastical causes (the Judicial Committee of the Privy Council) are not required to be Anglicans yet are required to deal with matters of theology as well as of liturgy.

These anachronisms have led to speculations concerning the future position of Church and State, for while in practice they have hitherto not come very greatly into conflict, this state of affairs could, in certain circumstances, be considerably changed. The latest report by a Commission of the Church Assembly on the subject foresees two possible choices, viz.: (1) Disestablishment, or (2) a revision of the terms of the establishment.

Disestablishment commends itself to some, but by no means to all. The advantages are to be considered against the disadvantages, and it is possible that the latter might in practice outweigh the former. Let us attempt to make a rough assessment.

A disestablished Church would be in a position to appoint the Bishops of its own choice. It would be able to order and change its own Prayer Book without reference to Parliament. Its rites and ceremonies would be for it to decide. It would be the ultimate authority on questions of theology, liturgy and discipline, and so able the more easily to rid itself of undesirable members both among the clergy and the laity.

On the other hand, disestablishment would almost inevitably mean a measure of disendowment which might well tend to hinder and limit the Church's evangelistic work. It might mean that one party within the Church became completely dominant over others. Its effect outside this country would be to suggest that Christianity had lost its influence rather more than was previously thought! It would make the attempt to convert the unconverted and re-convert the lapsed more difficult.

As Dr. William Temple (1881–1944) wrote in *Christianity*

and the State (1928) the fundamental question is not one of establishment at all:

> . . . the fundamental question is the right of an association within the Community to live its own life. The State is, of necessity, the only Authority which can determine to whom property belongs; it has not only the right, but the duty, to do this. If the Church were disestablished it still would not be effectively free if all the instruments of its work—its buildings and the like—were tied up by a Trust Deed to a particular system of doctrine. The great legal case affecting the Free Church of Scotland illustrates this. The House of Lords held in effect that the property of the Free Church of Scotland did not belong to a living body which, because living, might change its opinions, but to certain opinions of which the supporters were so few that they were known as the 'Wee Frees'; and Parliament had to pass special legislation to remedy a situation so manifestly absurd. It is this indefeasible supremacy of the State in questions of property which gives to the perennial problem of the relations of Church and State its abiding interest. Can there be living societies within the Community? It is by its strenuous insistence that there can be that the Church has rendered its most conspicuous service to the cause of liberty.

A revision of the terms of the existing establishment has already been discussed by the Convocations of Canterbury and York on the lines of the report by a Commission of the Church Assembly on Church and State (1952).

The suggestions made are such as to free the Church in certain ways while still maintaining its link with the State.

With regard to the appointment of bishops the proposals are that (1) the Prime Minister should continue to advise the Sovereign, after having consulted with the Archbishops; (2) at the option of the Archbishops a small committee of bishops, clergy and laity should be formed as a consultative body; (3) cathedral chapters should be allowed to petition the Crown for licence to elect and to represent at the same time the type of bishop deemed suitable for the needs of the diocese concerned; (4) the penalties liable to be inflicted upon a dean and chapter refusing to elect the Crown's nominee should be abolished.

Concerning church courts, it is suggested (1) that the Judicial Committee of the Privy Council should no longer be the final court of appeal in ecclesiastical matters; (2) the consistory court should be the only diocesan court, and the provincial courts should be limited to three, i.e. the court of the province, the court set up under the Benefices Act, 1898, and the Commission under the Bishops (Retirement) Measure, 1951; (3) appeals from the consistory court should be to the court of the province, with one exception; (4) new procedure to be adopted in doctrinal and ritual cases.

The proposed changes in, and additions to, the Prayer Book that the Commission considers should be deemed to be made by 'lawful authority' are:

1. Public services for special occasions and alterations in the State prayers, enjoined or authorized by royal warrant.

2. Changes made by statute before the canon is approved and changes made after by the Measure of the Church Assembly. (This provision retains the right of Parliament to legislate and to veto Measures of the Church Assembly.)

3. Experimental and optional deviations, authorized by the Convocation of Canterbury and York within their respective provinces, provided that nothing is contrary to the doctrine of the Church of England, and that no sanction shall be given without a majority of at least two-thirds of each House of Convocation and of the House of Laity.

4. Prayers and forms of service sanctioned by the bishop for which no provision is made in the Prayer Book, but subject to regulations which may be made by the Convocations.

5. Minor and unimportant variations in the conduct of public prayer made by the minister in his discretion according to particular circumstances. The purpose here

is to cover such as may occur in, say, a 'Mothering Sunday' Service.

4. *Church of England Schools*

There are to-day two types of Church of England school: the Controlled and the Aided.

In the case of the Controlled school, the State is financially responsible for it, but the buildings remain vested in ecclesiastical trustees. In the event of the school being re-built, the State appoints a large proportion of the managers and also the teachers. The incumbent, however, continues to be an *ex officio* manager.

Religious instruction is given to every child in the school except for those excused for reasons of conscience, and although the members of the staff need not be members of the Church of England, the incumbent and his curate (if any) may give such instruction, while in the larger schools Church of England teachers may be appointed to give such instruction in addition to their other teaching.

There are roughly 4,500 of such schools, and although from the Church's point of view the set-up is not altogether ideal, they still remain as Church schools.

The Aided schools, of which there are 3,378, receive grants from the State in part payment of the cost of outside repairs, improvements, development and rebuilding, the Church being responsible for 25 per cent of the whole cost. The majority of managers are appointed by the Church, and so are the teachers.

Sunday Schools

The Sunday School movement is usually attributed to Robert Raikes who, in 1780, together with a clergyman by the name of T. Stock, founded such a school at Gloucester, and gave considerable publicity to it in his

'Journal,' but in fact there had been other such schools initiated sporadically before that date.

These schools were designed not only to give religious instruction to children, but also to teach them to read and write, and for many of those who attended them they provided their sole education. In the *Memoirs of James Slade, Vicar of Bolton*, by Dr. Argles, Dean of Peterborough, we read: 'The instruction began with the Alphabet in the lowest class. There was no other School Elementary. The scholars attended regularly from ten to twenty years.'

By the early years of the next century, Sunday Schools were to be found all over England, few parishes being without one, and in 1803 the Sunday School Union was formed for the purpose of aiding such schools in the London area by supplying books, etc., while auxiliary bodies affiliated to the main Union were formed in other large centres.

There was, perhaps, a tendency in these schools to follow the well-known words (now usually omitted!) of a well-known hymn: 'The rich man in his castle, the poor man at his gate,' etc., etc. As Professor G. M. Trevelyan writes in his *English Social History*:

> In the early Nineteenth Century, the age of Hannah More, too much of the education and charity bestowed on the poor continued to be class-conscious and patronizing, when an equalitarian spirit unknown in the Eighteenth Century was beginning to render such anxious condescension unpalatable and out of touch with the needs and problems of a different age.
>
> 'God bless the Squire and his relations
> And keep us in our proper stations,'
>
> was a sentiment that scarcely aroused comment in the days of Sir Roger de Coverley, but this Sunday School attitude became a cause of scoffing and offence after the Industrial Revolution had put an end to the unconscious simplicity of traditional feudalism.

Nevertheless, while they doubtless reflected the prevailing attitude of the governing classes towards the others, it cannot be gainsaid that they were primarily concerned with teaching boys and girls the nature and meaning of the Word of God. Their primer was the Bible.

When general education began to increase, the teaching in Sunday Schools became almost entirely religious, and the numbers attending began to decline and have continued to do so, as have the numbers of teachers, in spite of the founding of a teachers' training college at Selly Oak, Birmingham, under the auspices of the Sunday School Union in 1907.

To-day there are in some parishes no Sunday Schools, and the statistics of Sunday School attendance leave no doubt that they are losing ground each year.

Geoffrey Gorer in *Exploring English Character* found that whereas 57 per cent of members of the Church of England send their children to Sunday Schools, 69 per cent of the Methodists do so, and even greater percentages of the Baptists, Congregationalists, Nonconformists and the small Protestant sects.

A recent writer on the subject[1] considers that the main reason for the decline is because

> . . . the Sunday Schools are not generally given the premier place, either in the parishes or in the policies of the Church, which their activities deserve. They are the Cinderellas, not only of Church education, but of all Church organizations. As a result there is a most serious shortage of teachers. In the two provinces there are only 77,710 Sunday School teachers. The measure of the decline may be gauged from the 'Barchester' diocese: in 1930 there were 4,000 teachers: in 1950 about 2,000. The drop is probably typical.

The same writer states that 'in the Ecclesiastical area of the Church of England there are about 1,048,000 Sunday School children.'

Cathedral Schools

These schools, originally established for the education of choirboys, continue to exist, but most of them now admit fee-paying pupils both as day-boys and boarders.

[1] *The Church of England*, by Guy Mayfield (1958).

CHAPTER TWO

THE CLERGY

THE Ministry is organized in three 'grades,' viz. Bishops, Priests and Deacons. These grades are considered to be of Divine, whereas various other orders are of ecclesiastical, origin.

There are in the Church of England two *Archbishops*, Canterbury and York.

The Archbishop of Canterbury is also the Primate of All England and the Archbishop of York is the Primate of England. They sign themselves Cantuar and Ebor prefaced by their first Christian name, respectively. They are also known as Metropolitans, indicating the exercise of provincial, and not merely diocesan, powers. In order of precedence in the State, the Archbishop of Canterbury comes immediately after the Sovereign and the Royal Dukes, and is followed by the Lord High Chancellor, after whom comes the Archbishop of York. It is the privilege of the Archbishop of Canterbury to crown the Sovereign, while the Archbishop of York may crown a Queen Consort, although usually Canterbury crowns both.

Both Archbishops are the respective guardians of the spiritualities of any vacant diocese within their provinces, and the Archbishop of Canterbury may grant special licences to marry, which are valid in both provinces, appoint notaries public, who may practise in both provinces, and grant degrees in divinity, arts, law and medicine, which are known as Lambeth degrees. On rare occasions he may exercise his right of visitation and deprivation of inferior bishops.

Archbishops are appointed by the Sovereign on the advice of the Prime Minister who, in practice, would consult persons of standing in the Church before tendering his advice. They have seats in the House of Lords as Spiritual Peers, and are styled: The Most Reverend His Grace the Lord Archbishop of ——, and addressed as 'My Lord Archbishop,' or 'Your Grace.'

Bishops

There are forty-one Diocesan Bishops[1] and forty-three Suffragans. They are nominally appointed by the Sovereign, but, in practice, by the Prime Minister, and after appointment are consecrated as Bishops of the Church and not of any particular diocese, but are then enthroned in the cathedral of their diocese.

As spiritual peers they have a limited number of seats in the House of Lords, the number being twenty-six, of which the Bishops of London, Durham and Winchester automatically take three while the remainder are filled according to seniority of consecration.[2] They are addressed as 'My Lord,' and have the style: The Right Reverend the Lord Bishop of ——, which is extended to all, whether Diocesan or Suffragans, by courtesy. In order of precedence they come immediately before Barons.

The word 'bishop' is an Anglo-Saxon corruption of 'episcopus,' meaning an overseer. Their special powers distinguishing them from priests are the conferring of Holy Orders and the administering of the rite of Confirmation.

The insignia of a bishop are the rochet, the chimere, and the episcopal throne which is usually situated on the gospel (north) side of the chancel of the cathedral church. The rochet is a white linen vestment with wide sleeves secured at the wrist by bands of black, and the chimere (worn over the rochet) is a silk or satin gown without sleeves.

In addition, bishops on occasions wear a cope and mitre, the latter being a shield-shaped hat with two fringed lappets hanging down at the back. They also have

[1] For details, see Chapter on Administration.
[2] Sodor and Man is also automatic, but has no vote.

a pastoral staff, called a crosier (crook-shaped), symbol of the spiritual shepherd of his people, a pectoral cross, and a special ring worn on the third finger of the right hand.

The Suffragan Bishoprics now in existence (1960) are:

	Diocese of—		Diocese of—
Dover	Canterbury	Reading	Oxford
Croydon		Buckingham	
Maidstone		Dorchester	
Willesden	London	Tonbridge	Rochester
Kensington		Bedford	St. Albans
Stepney		Dunwich	St. Edmundsbury and Ipswich
Fulham		Sherborne	Salisbury
Southampton	Winchester	Kingston-on-Thames	Southwark
Taunton	Bath and Wells	Woolwich	
Aston	Birmingham	Hull	York
Malmesbury	Bristol	Selby	
Colchester	Chelmsford	Whitby	
Barking		Jarrow	Durham
Lewes	Chichester	Lancaster	Blackburn
Crediton	Exeter	Burnley	
Plymouth		Penrith	Carlisle
Tewkesbury	Gloucester	Stockport	Chester
Stafford	Lichfield	Warrington	Liverpool
Shrewsbury		Hulme	Manchester
Grimsby	Lincoln	Middleton	
Grantham		Knaresborough	Ripon
Thetford	Norwich	Pontefract	Wakefield

There are also a number of 'retired' bishops, some of whom assist their diocesan brothers or act in some other ecclesiastical capacity. Colonial bishops do not come within the scope of this book.

Deans

The word dean derives from the Latin 'decanus,' originally meaning one having authority over ten, e.g. a monk having charge of ten others.

There are various types of dean, such as a Rural Dean; the Dean of the Arches; the heads of the collegiate churches of Westminster, Windsor and some other 'peculiars' which are independent of episcopal authority; the Dean of the Province of Canterbury who is Bishop of London *ex officio*. But here we are concerned with Deans of Cathedrals.

The Dean is the head of the Cathedral Chapter and virtually independent of the Diocesan Bishop, to whom he is next in rank. His duties are to control the Services in the Cathedral, and, together with the Chapter, to supervise its fabric and its finances. Deans are appointed by the Crown, and are usually selected from men of learning. They are styled the 'Very Reverend' and referred to as 'Mr. Dean' in conversation. It is worthy of note that the Dean of Christ Church, Oxford, is both head of the College and Dean of the Cathedral.

Archdeacons

Archdeacons are priests to whom a definite administrative authority in part of a Diocese has been delegated by the Bishop, and are called by the name of the territory so assigned, e.g. Archdeacon of Bath. They are styled 'Venerable' and referred to as 'Mr. Archdeacon' in conversation.

Their appointment is by the Diocesan Bishop and they form a useful link between the latter and his clergy. Their duties are various, among them being to make annual visitation within their Archdeaconries, being especially concerned with church fabric, and to admit churchwardens to office. They present candidates for ordination to the Bishop and induct clergy into the temporalities of their benefices. The two senior Archdeacons in each Diocese are *ex officio* members of the Convocation of their respective provinces, and all Archdeacons are *ex officio* members of their Diocesan Conference. To become an Archdeacon a priest must have been ordained for six years.

Provosts

A Provost was originally an official whose duty it was to look after land and rents belonging to a Cathedral or other institution, but now the title indicates one who is equivalent in the newer dioceses to a Dean in the older ones. Thus, whereas, e.g., Carlisle has its Dean, Bradford has its Provost. In the newer dioceses the Cathedral is also a parish church, and the Provost is also an incumbent with a cure of souls. He, like a Dean, is styled 'Very Reverend' and is referred to as 'Mr. Provost' in conversation. His duties are similar to those of a Dean. Appointment is by the Crown.

The title is also used in a non-ecclesiastical sense for the head of certain colleges, e.g. Oriel, Oxford; King's, Cambridge; and Eton.

Canons

There are three types of Canons: Residentiary, Non-Residentiary or Honorary, and Minor.

Residentiary Canons are those who have a 'prebend' in a Cathedral or Collegiate Church—a 'prebend' meaning part of the revenue as stipend. They are appointed by the Crown, the Lord Chancellor, an Archbishop, or the Bishop of a Diocese. In the older Dioceses there are usually three or four residentiary canons, but in the newer ones there is often only one and sometimes none, according to whether an endowment exists for a chapter. Residentiary Canons live within the Cathedral precincts and their duties are to preach in the Cathedral and other churches in the diocese, and, as part of the permanent staff, to be responsible for the maintenance of the Cathedral services, the fabric, etc. They also have the right of electing (or refusing to elect) the Crown's nominee to a vacant episcopal see, but in practice refusal does not occur.

Their mode of address is the Rev. Canon —— and in conversation they are referred to as Canon.

Honorary Canons are *Non-residentiary* and do not hold a salaried post, but have certain privileges and responsibilities. Their title is conferred on them by the Diocesan Bishop as a mark of distinction and their numbers vary in each Diocese. In some of the newer Cathedrals Honorary Canons are sometimes appointed to act as a Cathedral body. They are addressed in the same way as Residentiary Canons. Retired Honorary Canons are called Hon. Canons Emeriti (honourably discharged from service).

Minor Canons are appointed by the Dean and Chapter of a Cathedral mainly to sing services in the Cathedral. They are not members of the Chapter.

Prebendaries

In some Cathedrals (i.e. those belonging to the old Foundation, e.g. Exeter, St. Paul's, etc.) non-residentiary Canons are by custom entitled Prebendaries.

Priests

From very early times a Minister in the Church, other than a bishop or a deacon, was called a 'presbyter' from which the word 'priest' is derived.

In a wide sense of the word all ordained ministers of the Church of England, other than deacons, are priests, but here we are concerned with those who are not Bishops, Deans, Provosts, Archdeacons, or Canons. In other words, the bulk of the clergy.

As a rule they are either Rectors, Vicars, or Curates-in-charge of a parish, or are assistant curates to a Rector or Vicar.

The terms Rector and Vicar can only be explained historically. Originally the incumbent of the Parish

Church was called the Rector, and had the full rights to all tithes arising in his parish. The monasteries, however, pursued a policy of annexing many of the benefices, when they were said to have 'appropriated' the living. When this happened they took the living for their own use, but were bound to provide for the performance of services in the Church, and this they did by appointing a Minister to perform these services, and this Minister was known as the Vicar. Later, these Vicars were endowed with a portion of the glebe and a particular share of the tithes of the parish, usually called the 'small tithes,' the appropriators retaining the 'great tithes.' In this way arose our modern Vicarages. Since the tithes were taken over by the Government under the Tithes Acts of 1918 and 1936, the terms have ceased to have any real meaning, although they continue to be retained. Rectors, Vicars and Curates-in-charge are all known as Incumbents of their benefices and their duties are laid down in the Ordination Service in the Book of Common Prayer, and may be summed up as being to show proper respect for their office and due solicitude for the moral and spiritual welfare of their parishioners.

Once installed, the incumbent has entire control of the arrangements for Divine Services, but must comply with the provisions of the Book of Common Prayer. He must hold morning and evening services on Sundays and certain Holy Days, but the times fixed for such services are matters for him to decide. He must celebrate the Holy Communion as directed by the Prayer Book, but the frequency of celebrations is within his discretion. He may direct the music and singing. In practice it is usual for him to consult his Churchwardens and his Parochial Church Council with regard to times of services, etc.

The parsonage house and any glebe land are vested in him, and it is his duty to reside within his parish. Unless he is found guilty of certain misdeeds, an incumbent cannot be deprived of his benefice, but he may resign, exchange or receive promotion which will render the benefice vacant. None of his stipend is received from the State.

Deacons

The Diaconate forms the lowest rank in the Christian Ministry, and it is, therefore, as a Deacon that a cleric begins his ministerial work. He is bound (unless the Bishop shall decree otherwise) to remain in that office for a whole year, and during it he is debarred from giving private Absolution and from pronouncing the General Absolution and the Blessing. Candidates for the Diaconate must be twenty-three years old, and must satisfy the Bishop as to their intellectual, moral and spiritual fitness for the office.

At the service of Holy Communion a Deacon may not consecrate the elements, but may read the Gospel (his proper duty), and may hand the chalice and assist the celebrating Priest as directed. In general, his duties are to assist the Priest to whose parish he has been appointed.

Chaplains

Chaplains are priests who perform non-parochial duties, and there are various types of them: Chaplains to the Sovereign, to Bishops and to noblemen; those appointed to serve in H.M. armed forces; those appointed to serve in such institutions as schools and colleges, prisons, workhouses, cemeteries, hospitals and parliament; Chaplains to certain Embassies in foreign countries (e.g. France, U.S.S.R., Spain, etc.); and examining Chaplains to Bishops.

When Chaplains are appointed by the State they are paid by the State; in other cases they are paid by their particular employers.

Various

Parson. Originally the parson was one who was entitled to full possession of the rights of a benefice (i.e.

rector), but in common usage it denotes any clergyman.

A *Squarson*, of whom there are very few to-day, is the nickname given to an incumbent who is also the Squire of the Parish.

Surrogate

The term indicates a clergyman, or other person, appointed by the Bishop as his deputy to grant licences for marriages without banns.

Precentor

He is responsible for the direction of the choral services in a Cathedral. It is to be noted, however, that by no means every Cathedral appoints one.

Proctor

A proctor is a representative of the diocesan clergy in convocation.

The title '*Reverend*' was first used before a priest's name in the fifteenth century, and is a courtesy title.

Dress of the Clergy

The official dress of clergymen is distinctive both outside as well as inside a church, but there has been a marked tendency in recent years for many of them, especially when away from their parishes or off duty, to dress like any other men. This is easily accomplished by substituting for the clerical collar and black stock, which is often the sole distinctive feature of his dress, an ordinary collar and tie as worn by the non-clerical!

This clerical collar has, incidentally, only been in use for about a hundred years, and is derived from the high white stock regularly worn during the eighteenth and early part of the nineteenth centuries by clergy and laity alike.

Certain dignitaries of the Church have distinctive articles of dress, apart from their collars. Thus Bishops, Deans and Archdeacons wear breeches and gaiters, aprons, and a sort of frock coat. In the case, too, of a Bishop, the stock is purple and he wears a pectoral cross. But even these dignitaries are inclined when *en vacances* to doff these garments and to appear as other men! The apron is really a shortened form of cassock, reaching to the knees, and the gaiters are a survival after the introduction of trousers. Official hats are in every case black, as are the other items of dress, except the purple stock already referred to, and they frequently have certain adornments in the shape of strings and rosettes to indicate the rank of the wearer. Some clergymen wear a cassock when going about among their parishioners.

Most of the clergy are clean-shaven and beards are now seldom to be seen. Moustaches usually indicate very Protestant views!

So much for clerical dress when the wearer is not taking part in Church Services. When he is, he wears a variety of articles according to his rank, to the particular Service in which he is taking part, and to his Churchmanship, i.e. High or Low Church. Here is a list of the various garments:

Cassock—Black in colour, except for Bishops when it is purple, it is a long black garment, with sleeves, reaching from the neck to the ankle and secured round the middle with a belt. Sometimes it has a sort of short cape round the shoulders.

Surplice—White, made of linen, and with wide sleeves, it hangs from the shoulders in varying lengths, but is not as long as a cassock.

Cassocks and surplices are also worn by choirmen and choirboys, by servers and by lay-readers, and have no symbolical significance.

Alb—A white linen or silk garment with tight-fitting sleeves. Secured round the waist by a girdle, and reaching to the ankle, it is worn by priests at the Holy Communion. It now symbolizes purity, but began its life as a first-century Roman gentleman's ordinary dress.

Stole—A strip of silk about eight feet long and four inches wide, worn round the neck with each end hanging straight down on either side, except (*a*) when worn with certain other Eucharistic vestments its ends are crossed over the breast; and (*b*) when used by a deacon it is worn over the left shoulder, like a sash, with its ends fastened together under the right arm. It is of different colours according to the occasion. And simple though it is, it is the essential 'priestly' vestment.

Scarf—A black scarf considerably wider than a stole and worn round the neck with the ends hanging straight down on either side in front.

Chasuble—A vestment of varying colour worn as the outer garment by the celebrant at a Holy Communion Service. It is usually shield-shaped, with an opening for the head, and is sleeveless. It has become more common in the Church of England since the Oxford Movement, having fallen into disuse.

Maniple—a strip of silk about a yard long and four to five inches wide worn over the left arm by the celebrant at the Holy Communion. It is of different colours, and often carries three crosses.

Cope—This is a long sleeveless semi-circular cloak worn on certain festival occasions instead of a chasuble. It is of different colours, and often magnificently embroidered. At the back, below the neck, it has a triangular-shaped ornament which was originally a hood.

Amice—a square of white linen, originally worn on the head, but now round the neck of the celebrant at Holy Communion.

Biretta—a hard square cap. For priests it is coloured black, and for bishops purple. There is also the *Canterbury Cap* which is a similar sort of head-dress but of soft material.

Bands—these are part of academic dress, and are also worn by lawyers. They are derived from the flat starched collars, which superseded the ruff in the seventeenth century.

Training for the Ministry

In order to enter the Ministry it is necessary for the candidate to be a baptized and confirmed male member of the Church. He must be of good moral character, not less than twenty-three years of age, and have certain educational qualifications.

The Central Advisory Council of Training for the Ministry (known as 'Cactum,' C.A.C.T.M.), established in 1912, is the body concerned with such candidates.

Its functions are:

1. To watch the supply of candidates for Holy Orders, and its sources.
2. To consider the best methods of training and testing candidates, and to control the General Ordination Examination.
3. To provide for the inspection of Theological Colleges and any other institutions offering similar preparation to candidates for Holy Orders; and to advise as to the formation and supply of new Theological Colleges.
4. To receive money in order to finance individual candidates, and make grants in aid of Diocesan Ordination Candidates Funds and other bodies engaged in the work of preparing candidates for Ordination.
5. Generally to promote unity of action between all those concerned in the training of candidates for Holy Orders, and to collect information and make suggestions for the guidance of the Bishops.

Before candidates are selected for a recognized course of training they are required to have passed an examination of matriculation standard, or to be qualified for a course of training approved by the Bishops. They must also pass such medical examination as C.A.C.T.M. shall prescribe and attend a Selection Board.

The method of the Selection Boards is to hold conferences lasting three days, in various centres, to which are invited about twenty candidates and five selectors. These selectors are appointed by the Diocesan Bishops, and include laymen. Each candidate is seen separately by each of the selectors, and their opinions as to his true vocation are pooled.

After having been selected as suitable, a candidate has to undergo training according to his age. Thus all those of the age of thirty or under are normally required, either to obtain a University degree which shall be followed by two years' post-graduate theological, pastoral and devotional training, including residence at a recognized Theological College, and to pass the General Ordination Examination or its equivalent, or, if a University Course is not recommended, to take a course of three or four years' training at a recognized Theological College or under some other authority approved by the Bishops in consultation with C.A.C.T.M. and to pass the General Ordination Examination or its equivalent.

If a candidate is aged forty, or over, he is required to follow such courses of theological, pastoral and devotional training as shall be prescribed by the Bishop.

Finance naturally plays an important part in the training, and as comparatively few candidates are to-day in a position to finance themselves, the Central Board of Finance of the Church of England provides large sums to aid them. Help is also given by the State and by Local Education Authorities.

Theological Colleges

There are twenty-six Theological Colleges with a total accommodation for roughly fourteen hundred candidates, and fees varying from £270 to £160 per annum, the average being between £200 and £250. The oldest existing of these is Queen's College, Birmingham, founded in 1828, and the most recent are Clifton Theological College, Bristol, and Oak Hill College, Southgate, both of which were founded in 1932.

In addition to these Theological Colleges there is Brasted Place in Kent, where a special residential course is available for selected candidates who would profit by a year of pre-theological training.

Principal Theological Colleges

- St. Aidan's, Birkenhead
- Queen's College, Birmingham
- Clifton Theological College, Stoke Bishop, Bristol
- Ridley Hall, Cambridge
- Westcott House, Cambridge
- Bishops' College, Cheshunt
- Theological College, Chichester
- Tyndale Hall, Clifton
- Theological College, Cuddesdon
- St. Chad's College, Durham
- St. John's College, Durham
- Theological College, Ely
- House of the Sacred Mission, Kelham
- Theological College, Lichfield
- Lincoln Theological College, Lincoln
- King's College, London
- London College of Divinity, Northwood, Middlesex
- College of the Resurrection, Mirfield
- Ripon Hall, Oxford
- St. Stephen's House, Oxford
- Wycliffe Hall, Oxford
- Theological College, Salisbury
- Oak Hill Theological College, Southgate
- St. Boniface College, Warminster
- Theological College, Wells
- Worcester Ordination College

Ordination

When a candidate for ordination has passed the necessary tests and the Diocesan Bishop considers him to be a fit and proper person to enter the Ministry, he is made a Deacon. This is performed by the Bishop after the candidate has been presented to him by the Archdeacon, or his deputy.

The form of Service is to be found in the Book of Common Prayer and takes place on a Sunday or Holy Day.

A deacon has to remain in that office for a full year (unless otherwise so ordered by the Bishop), and is then ordained a priest. This ceremony is also performed by the Bishop, and the form of service is likewise to be found in the Book of Common Prayer.

Note on the Supply of Clergy

There has been a noticeable and grievous decline in numbers of the clergy during recent years. According to Dr. Cyril Garbett's *In an Age of Revolution*, there were, in 1905, irrespective of those who had retired, 19,053 clergymen in the two provinces of Canterbury and York; in 1914 there were 18,180; in 1930 there were 16,745; in 1941, 17,001; and in 1949, 14,380. In 1937 there were 558 ordained to the diaconate, in 1939, 589 and in 1950, 419. Since then the numbers have somewhat increased, and in 1959 there were, according to the *Church of England Year Book*, 512. Nevertheless, in view of the increase in the population of the country, there is still a sorry shortage and the traditional parochial system, by which every parish small or great had its own incumbent, can no longer be maintained, while in the larger towns there are parishes containing many thousands of people with only one clergyman to minister to them.

Various methods by which the services of those clergy that there are may be best utilized, such as the union of two or more benefices, have been outlined in an earlier part of this book, but it is devoutly to be hoped that more men may think fit, and prove fit, to be ordained.

Institution and Induction

There are two ceremonies which take place in connection with the incumbent of a benefice, namely institution and induction.

By the process of *institution* a clergyman is placed in possession of the 'spiritualities' of the benefice. In other words, the cure of souls in the parish is placed in his hands. This is always performed by a Bishop and (unlike an induction) may take place anywhere the Bishop so desires. Before institution, notice of the intention to institute is sent to the Churchwardens and affixed to the church door, where it must remain for the kalendar month. In addition, the prospective incumbent must assent to the Thirty-nine Articles and the Book of Common Prayer, make a declaration against simony[1] and take oaths of allegiance to the Sovereign and of canonical obedience to the Bishop.

By *induction* a clergyman is placed in possession of the 'temporalities' (as opposed to the 'spiritualities') of the benefice, which means that he is given legal right to receive certain revenues, and possession of the church building and the parsonage house. The ceremony of induction is performed by the Archdeacon, acting on a mandate from the Bishop, or by the Rural Dean or some other clergyman, acting on a precept from the Archdeacon. It usually takes place in the parish church and certain ceremonies, such as tolling the bell, form part of it.

Patronage

Before he can be instituted and inducted into a benefice the incumbent must be appointed to it, and this right of appointment is called an advowson. The patron possessing this right may be another cleric, or a layman, or a corporation recognized by the law. In those cases, and there are many of them, where the Diocesan Bishop has himself the right of appointment no further steps need to be taken,[2]

[1] Simony is the corrupt presentation of any person to an ecclesiastical benefice for money, gift or reward. It is a purely ecclesiastical offence, and not punishable by the criminal law.

[2] The clergyman is said to be 'collated' to the benefice.

but in the others the patrons must present the nominee for institution to the Bishop, since they do not possess the right of putting their candidate in spiritual, or legal, possession of the benefice themselves. Moreover, the Bishop may reject the candidate, but will not do so unless he has some legal reason for so doing, and, in practice, patrons often consult the Diocesan Bishop before presenting a candidate.

The right of advowson may be held by anyone who is not a Roman Catholic, an alien, or a lunatic, and the right may be transferred by gift or sale, since in English law it is treated as a right of property.

In the event of a patron failing to present a candidate within six kalendar months of the vacancy arising, his right is said to lapse and passes to the Bishop, and if the same situation occurs with the Bishop it passes to the Archbishop, and if yet again the Archbishop fails to present, it passes to the Crown. But such instances are rare.

The following are some of the patrons of livings:

- Archbishops of Canterbury and York
- Diocesan Bishops
- Deans and Chapters of Cathedrals
- Universities, Colleges and Schools
- Large landowners and other private individuals
- The Crown (First Lord of the Treasury or the Lord Chancellor)
- Diocesan Boards of Patronage
- Trustees (e.g. Hulme's, Peache, Simeon's)
- Church Society Trust
- Church Patronage Society
- Church Pastoral-Aid Society
- Incumbents of other parishes
- Community of the Resurrection, Mirfield
- Chancellor of the Duchy of Lancaster
- The Duchy of Cornwall (exercised by the Duke)
- Home Secretary (Channel Islands and the living of Kirk Andreas, Isle of Man)
- Lieut.-Governor of Isle of Man (all other Isle of Man livings)

There are somewhere in the neighbourhood of 14,000 benefices.

In 1957 the undermentioned patrons had the right of presentation to the undermentioned livings:

The Crown		158 livings
The Queen		8 ,,
The Lord Chancellor		558 ,,
The Home Secretary		41 ,,
The Duchy of Lancaster		42 ,,
The Duchy of Cornwall		26 ,,
The Admiralty		8 ,,
The Diocesan Bishops	about	3,000 ,,
Parochial Clergy	,,	1,200 ,,
Diocesan Boards of Patronage ..	,,	200 ,,

Purely ecclesiastical patrons present to under one-third of the benefices!

The Parson's Freehold

By the term 'parson's freehold' is meant the fact that the incumbent of a parish cannot be removed from his benefice except after trial and conviction of an offence which carries this penalty.

In the words of Bishop Hensley Henson:[1]

the incumbent of an English parish enjoys a measure of independence in the exercise of his ministry which is probably both unprecedented and unparalleled. Neither the Roman priest nor the Protestant minister is so little controlled by authority as an Anglican parson, for while the priest is subject to the Bishop, and the minister to his Congregation, the parson, within the large limit of the law, which regards his cure of souls as his personal property, can ignore both.

The Bishop continues:

Whether wise and considerate, or tactless and unteachable, the incumbent will be singularly free from official interference. His position is almost impregnable, for he enjoys the freehold of his benefice. Whether he be conscientious, hard-working and respected, or indifferent, idle, and despised, his income is secure so long as he avoids conduct which shocks the public

[1] *The Church of England*, 1939.

conscience and compels episcopal action. His lawful authority is considerable and unquestioned. He has control of the hours of service, and his pastoral obligations are in practice determined by himself. His parochial church council can protest, denounce, and complain, but it can do little more. The rural dean may report; the Archdeacon may visit; the Bishop may direct, but neither rural dean, nor Archdeacon, nor even Bishop, can bring any effective remedy to indifference, idleness, and secularity. The extent of the English clergyman's legal obligation is curiously small: his pastoral duty is indeed solemn and absorbing, but he must needs be his own interpreter of its range and requirement. Legal securities against pastoral inefficiency are little likely to be effective in practice. . . . Expulsion from his benefice is the only remedy for proved pastoral inefficiency, and that is a remedy of such severity that it can only be fairly adopted when the legal rights of the individual have been carefully secured. It must always be remembered, that natural kindheartedness will generally disincline parishioners to assist any disciplinary action which will bear hardly, not merely on the incumbent, whom they may desire to get rid of, but on his wife and children, whom they may regard with affection and pity. His expulsion will bring them to destitution. It is hardly ever the reluctance of the bishop to exert his lawful powers in restraint of clerical fault that perpetuates even culpable inefficiency and gross personal ill-conduct in the parishes, but the refusal of the parishioners to attest the offences for which they so loudly complain. In *theory* the bishop's disciplinary power is very great: in *practice* it is extremely small, nor is it easy to see how it could be increased without violating principles of equity which the public conscience rightly holds in reverence. In really bad cases of moral delinquency, the bishop may and often does bring such pressure to bear on the incumbent as forces him to resign his benefice: but this extra-legal method is obviously open to grave objection, and may fail to succeed.

Since Bishop Henson wrote the above words a measure of the Church Assembly, designed to deal with the unworthy or inept parson, has been passed. Thus, under the Incumbents (Disability) Measure, 1945, the Bishop is empowered to convene a panel of clergy to inquire into a case where an incumbent is alleged to be incapable of performing his duties through disability arising from age or infirmity, whether bodily or mental.

Apart from this aspect of the 'parson's freehold' there is the material one, by which he is the limited owner, during his incumbency, of church, churchyard and parsonage house, subject to certain provisions and safeguards of ecclesiastical law. Thus he cannot arbitrarily be excluded from the church or churchyard, and therefore from the pulpit or prevented from carrying out his ministry. Similarly, he is for the time being the owner of the parsonage house in which, unless other accommodation be found and the bishop be willing for him to use it, he is compelled to reside.

The inherent weaknesses of the 'parson's freehold' are clear, and there is no doubt that situations arise in which it must be beneficial for all concerned if the removal of an unsatisfactory incumbent were to be made easier, but on the other hand it must not be forgotten that his duty is to preach Christian truth, however unpopular this may appear to his parishioners, and as a champion, which he should be, of moral and social righteousness he requires freedom of speech and action and this is guaranteed to him, without fear of persecution or of economic sanctions, by his 'freehold.'

CHAPTER THREE

THE LAITY

Rights of Parishioners

By the word 'laity' is meant all those members of the Church, other than the clergy. It is the duty of the laity to contribute to the support of the Church in various ways, not only by attending services, but also with gifts of money and by obedience to the clergy in spiritual matters. It is their right to look to the clergy for guidance and help, and for the performance of certain ministrations.

Every parishioner has the right of burial in the burial place of his own parish, i.e. where he resides, or where he owns rateable property. There are certain fees payable. The parish priest is also under an obligation to baptize parishioners, whether infants or adults, provided he receives proper notice. No fee or reward may be demanded either for the celebration of this sacrament or for the registering of it. In the case of marriage, a parishioner, above the age of sixteen, has the right to be married in his parish church or in the church in which he is accustomed to worship, i.e. the church on the electoral roll of which his name is entered. Certain fees are payable by him.

With regard to the electoral roll, a lay member of the Church is entitled to have his or her name entered on it provided he, or she, is seventeen years of age or upwards, is a baptized member of the Church of England, and declares that he, or she, does not belong to any religious body not in communion with that Church, is resident in the parish, or, if not so resident, has habitually attended public worship in the parish during a period of six months before enrolment and has signed the necessary form of application for enrolment.

A lay member has a right to a seat in his or her parish church provided there is one available.

Reference has already been made (*vide* chapter on Administration) to Parochial Church Councils, the Church Assembly, Ruri-decanal and Diocesan Conferences in all of which the laity are represented. In addition there are certain official or semi-official posts occupied by lay members in the Church, as follows.

READERS

The office of reader in its present form dates from 1866 and their number has gradually increased. Indeed, to-day, when there is such a shortage of clergy, readers are a very valuable asset to the Church and are welcomed by most incumbents.

In order to become a reader a candidate is required to be nominated by an Incumbent. After examination and having signed a declaration of loyalty to the doctrine of the Church of England and to the Bishop and the Incumbent, he is admitted to the office and given a copy of the New Testament. He also receives a certificate signed by the Bishop indicating his admission into the Lay Ministry. This certificate either confines his services to a particular parish or allows him to act as a reader anywhere within the Diocese. A reader in the Diocese is not, however, at liberty to serve as such in any other, except by permission of the Diocesan Bishop concerned.

The duties of a reader may include:

1. To visit the sick, to read and pray with them, to teach in Sunday School and elsewhere, and generally to undertake such pastoral and educational work, and to give such assistance to the Incumbent as he may direct.

2. To read Morning or Evening Prayer, to publish Banns of Marriage, to say the Litany, to read the Scriptures, to preach and give addresses except at the

Holy Communion, to catechize children in church. These duties he may perform in any consecrated building throughout the Diocese.

In addition, he may, but only on special occasions and with the authorization of the Bishop, read the Epistle and administer the Chalice at Holy Communion.

Readers do not receive any payment for their services, but in the event of their having to spend money on travelling such travelling expenses may be allowed to them by arrangement with the Incumbent of the particular parish in which they are serving. Moreover, when a reader serves in a parish other than his own, there is a fee payable by that parish to the Diocesan Readers' Board.

When serving in church a reader wears cassock, surplice, and a medallion suspended from a silk ribbon round his neck—the medallion and ribbon being provided by the Diocese.

Each Diocese has a Readers' Board and these Boards are co-ordinated by the Central Readers' Board, which consists of the Archbishops, four Bishops, six representatives from each Diocese, and not more than twelve co-opted members.

Churchwardens

It is the general practice nowadays for the Incumbent to elect one Churchwarden and the Parishioners the other, or others, for there may be more than two, according to custom in the parish. The elections take place annually, and usually at the Easter Vestry and Parochial Church Electors joint meeting, except in the case of new parishes when it must be within two months from the date when the parish is formed. Churchwardens, although thus elected, may not act as such until they have been admitted by the Archdeacon, or his deputy. Women are eligible as well as men, and all Churchwardens are equal in status and are legally officers of the Bishop.

It is customary for them to occupy special seats in church and to have a ceremonial staff, in the shape of a long stick surmounted by a small silver or brass cross.

Their duties are to help in the organization of all activities connected with the church in the parish, to arrange for the collection of alms, to attend to the seating arrangements and the behaviour and comfort of worshippers, but, since the establishment of Parochial Church Councils in 1921, they share many other of their previous duties with all the members of the P.C.C.

For further details, *A Handbook for Churchwardens and Parochial Church Councillors* (Mowbrays, 5*s.*) is recommended.

Sidesmen

The word 'sidesmen' is an abbreviated form of 'synodsmen,' i.e. laymen chosen to attend the diocesan synod for the purpose of answering questions relating to the parishes they represented.

Sidesmen to-day are elected annually by the Parochial Church Meeting and may be male or female and in number according to the needs and custom of the particular parish. In order to be elected they must be on the Electoral Roll.

They act as deputies of the Churchwardens, and in practice their main duty is the collecting of alms at services.

Organists and Choirs

The organist is engaged by the Incumbent, and the direction and control of him, so far as Church Services are concerned, are his alone. With regard to any payment made to him, it is the duty of the Parochial Church Council to supply the necessary funds, and sometimes a definite contract between organists, incumbent and P.C.C. is drawn up. Similarly this is the case with a paid choir.

The organist should not only devote himself to performing his part in services devoutly and to the best of his ability, but should abide by the decision of the Incumbent as to what parts of it shall be musically rendered. He is also responsible for recruiting the choir.

In some churches the choir wear cassocks and surplices. The cassocks may be of any colour, but by custom scarlet is reserved for choristers in the Chapels Royal and churches of Royal Foundation.

Vergers

Vergers are those who look after the interior of a church in order to keep it clean and in proper order for services. In some churches it is customary for them to wear a black gown. The word 'verger'[1] strictly means one who carries a verge, or mace, before a dignitary, and often it is the verger who leads a procession in church, in order to clear the way, which was more necessary in bygone days than it is now, because there were then no pews or chairs, and the congregation stood where they pleased, Vergers are still found in the larger churches, but their number is on the decrease. There is a Church of England Guild of Vergers.

Servers

A server, either an adult male or a boy, is one who at a Holy Communion Service assists the Celebrant in certain ways by moving the altar-book from side to side as required, saying certain responses, receiving the offertory, ringing the Sanctus bell, and helping with the ablutions. He wears a cassock and surplice.

Thurifers

A thurifer is a person who at religious ceremonies carries a thurible, or censer, containing incense. This vessel is usually of silver and suspended on chains from

[1] Sometimes spelt 'virger.'

which the thurifer can swing it. He is often attended by a small boy, known as a 'boat boy,' on account of his bearing the incense-boat. Both thurifer and boat-boy wear cassock and short surplice. It is customary for the boat-boy to be of diminutive size.

Lay Rectors

A person, other than the clergy, who receives tithes, or their equivalent since tithe was taken over by the government, is known as a lay rector, and has the right to the chief seat in the chancel of the church concerned. He is also responsible for the upkeep of the chancel, but may compound for this liability with the Diocesan Board of Finance.

The title came into being after the Reformation when King Henry VIII dissolved the monasteries and granted certain tithes they held to lay persons.

Sacristan

The official who has charge of the contents of a church may be either a man or a woman, appointed by the parish priest, especially to look after the sacred vessels, vestments, etc. It is almost invariably undertaken voluntarily and has no legal basis.

Diocesan Chancellor

The Chancellor is the Bishop's Official and Vicar-General, and is the principal lay officer in the Diocese, holding his office 'for life.' He is usually the President of the Consistory Court, and acts as legal and administrative adviser to the Bishop. He hears applications for faculties, dispensations, etc., and is responsible for fixing fees in new parishes. He also issues marriage licences through his surrogates.

Deaconesses

The Order of Deaconesses was formally restored by the Convocation of Canterbury in 1923, and by that of

York in 1925. In her ordination, a deaconess is dedicated to life-long service, but such services vary from place to place, and are not specifically defined. In order to qualify as a Deaconess a candidate must be at least twenty-three years old, have passed a selection board, and undergone training at a residential college for two years.

The first deaconess in the Church of England was 'dedicated' in 1861. There are now about two hundred at work in England.

Diocesan Surveyor

Every Diocese has one or more architect and surveyor who advises in connection with the fabric of ecclesiastical buildings.

The Duties of Church Membership

What is expected of lay members of the Church of England? Here are six rules compiled by the Convocations of Canterbury and York.

1. To pray every day and read the Bible regularly.
2. To join in the worship of the Church every Sunday, and to observe Holy Days.
3. To receive the Holy Communion regularly after due preparation and more particularly at the great Festivals of the Church and on the great occasions of their own lives.
4. To mark Fridays, and the season of Lent, by special acts of devotion and self-denial.
5. To contribute worthily to the work of the Church at home and overseas, and for the relief of those in need.
6. To uphold the marriage laws of the Church, and to bring up children to love and serve the Lord.

Hats in Church for Women

St. Paul in his 1st Epistle to the Corinthians (xi. 4–5) wrote: 'Every man praying or prophesying, having his head covered, dishonoureth his head. But every woman that prayeth or prophesieth with her head uncovered dishonoureth her head.'

Up to the 1939–45 War it was almost universal for women to cover their heads in church, but the custom has changed to a limited extent and many of the younger members of the female sex now attend services with their heads uncovered.

There is no ecclesiastical objection to this, as Archbishop William Temple pointed out, and while it may, and certainly does, offend the prejudices of some, there is no reason to suppose that the object of the hatless is other than to do what pleases them and so far as they know does not offend Almighty God!

The Layman looks at the Clergy

To many—perhaps the majority—of lay people the clergyman's job is regarded as being 'cushy.' They may like him, personally, or they may not; but it is doubtful, by and large, whether he commands much respect by virtue of his office alone, and such authority as he at one time possessed has gone or is largely going. They regard much of what he tells them as poppy-cock! They say that he never visits them, or, on the contrary, is too often on the door-step! They compare him with his predecessor, and after a short while wish the latter was back again! They find him in the 'local' and, although he drinks his half-pint and plays darts with them, somehow there is a feeling of relief when he departs. He makes them feel slightly awkward—they could not say exactly why or how, or they very definitely could and do! The deaf ones complain that they cannot hear what he says in church; the non-deaf wish that he would speak less loudly! They assert that he is more inclined to mix with the richer, rather than the poorer, element in the parish!

Much of this criticism levelled against the clergy is unfair, and those who voice it are biased for some reason, but it cannot be denied that, as in all human institutions, there are members of the priesthood (as there always have been and presumably always will be) who do not even nearly approximate to the ideal. On the other hand it must not be forgotten that there are many others whose ministrations to the communities they serve is in accord with the teaching of Him Whom they seek to represent.

CHAPTER FOUR

CHURCH SERVICES

Holy Communion

This is the Central Service of the Church, and is also known as the Eucharist, the Lord's Supper, and the Mass.

It originates from the Last Supper with His disciples which our Lord held in the upper room in Jerusalem before His Crucifixion and during which He brake bread and poured wine and gave it to them, saying: 'Take, eat, this is My Body which is given for you; do this in remembrance of Me,' and 'Drink ye all of this; for this is My Blood of the New Covenant, which is shed for you and for many for the remission of sins; do this, as oft as ye shall drink it, in remembrance of Me.'

The service is either 'said' or 'sung,' according, as a rule, to the time of day when it is held. Thus early 'celebrations' are almost invariably said, while mid-morning ones are often sung with hymns and a sermon. In the majority of churches some years ago it was seldom 'sung,' but there is now a growing tendency towards holding what is known as a Parish Communion, while Anglo-Catholics have always made it the main service of each Sunday, celebrating it both early and later in the morning, said at the former time and sung at the latter.

There is a considerable diversity of opinion among the clergy, as well as the laity, concerning certain points of doctrine in connection with the nature of the elements in the Eucharist, but these are outside the scope of this little book.

As with most, if not all, Church of England services there is no complete uniformity in the Administration of Holy Communion. In some churches the old order of 1662 is observed, in others the alternative order of 1928, in others a sort of amalgamation of both, and in yet others a service which dates from medieval times, but for which in fact there is no authority to-day. But these last need not concern us here as they are comparatively few. The chief difference outwardly lies in the garments worn by the priest which may either be surplice and stole or a white alb with a chasuble.

Other differences are:

The Commandments—Instead of the Ten Commandments our Lord's Summary of the Law is often substituted, while in some churches the *Kyrie eleison* ('Lord, have mercy') takes the place of the Commandments.

Collect for the Queen—This is sometimes omitted.

Epistle—Sometimes referred to as the 'Lesson' and chanted.

Gospel—Chanted in some churches below the chancel.

Prayer for the Church—The words 'Militant here in earth' in the preface are sometimes omitted.

The Lord's Prayer, and the Prayer following it (1662)—These are now often prayed immediately after the Prayer of Consecration, and not after members of the congregation have communicated.

Agnus Dei ('O Lamb of God')—In some churches this is sung immediately before members of the congregation communicate.

Incense—In some churches incense is used.

Sacring, or Sanctus Bell—The bell is rung at the elevation of the host—a survival of the time when people who could no longer follow Latin were enabled to realize what was taking place.

Some of these acts of ritual depend upon whether the service is being said or sung.

A good description of High Mass in an Anglo-Catholic Church is to be found in *The Church of England in the Twentieth Century* by Roger Lloyd. After describing the sort of congregation to be found in 'the ancient parish of St. Boniface hard by the docks in any seaport in England at eleven o'clock on a Sunday morning,' he continues:

Behind the scenes in the vestries, there is controlled bustle. The servers in their scarlet cassocks appear with tapers to light the candles. The choir, a surprisingly large choir, struggles into cassocks and surplices. It talks much less than most choirs: the organist has no difficulty in getting attention for a last-minute message. In a corner a tall young man blows upon the ignited charcoal, and places it in the silver censer which is held for him by a midget of a child. All this is superintended by a middle-aged man, a lawyer, who is the Master of Ceremonies, and who obviously sets a very high value on his position. The priest is in his own vestry making himself ready. In a moment he will come out, vested, to the choir, where his six servers in their lace cottas will join him, and the processions of Entry—his own entry being separate from that of the choir and the curate—will be formed.

As soon as all are in their places, the procession proper begins. First comes the Cross-bearer, and then the young man with the incense, his left hand on the shoulder of the tiny boat-boy, his right hand swinging the censer by its long silver chain. Clouds of incense eddy softly at every step. He is followed by the choir-boys and men; and all, having been properly trained, bear their part with a deep reverence. Then come the servers, and finally the priest, wearing a cope heavy with magnificence, the ends of which are ceremoniously held clear of his walking feet by two little boys. As he passes down the aisle, the people in the nearest pews bow. Presently the procession winds back into the Chancel, and as the last verse of the hymn is sung, the priest's attendants divest him of his cope, and put on him his Eucharistic vestments. He then places more grains of incense into the censer, and the liturgy is ready to begin.

Here, too, every possible decoration and enhancement which the arts of music and visual image can provide is taken into use to honour the Sacrament and to teach the people. There is a ceremonial gospel procession with candles and incense. There are appropriate hymns. There is a Sermon. There is the solemn censing of priest, choir, preacher and people. At the supreme moment there is the Ceremony of the Kiss of Peace. Every detail has been lovingly cared for.

Nothing whatever has been left undone which might help to impress upon the people that this is the Service of services, and the church where in the Blessed Sacrament is none other than the Court of Heaven.

The use of Incense is one of the controversial subjects connected with the Administration of Holy Communion. To many members of the Church of England it is entirely a Roman practice, but in fact since the Reformation it was occasionally used in the Church of England between the sixteenth and nineteenth centuries. Not, however, until the Oxford Movement (1833–45) did it become at all frequent and even since then it is the exception rather than the rule to find it used in our churches. Nor has it ever received ecclesiastical authority, and when its 'legality' was argued before the Archbishops of Canterbury and York, in 1899, their *opinion* was that the liturgical use of it was illegal. Nevertheless, those members of the priesthood who argue that it is their duty to insist on its ceremonial use as a part of the Catholic practice of the Church of England continue to do so, while the Bishops as a whole seem neither to approve or disapprove!

It symbolizes the rising of prayer to God as is indicated in the Revelation of St. John the Divine (viii. 3, 4): 'And another angel came and stood over the altar, having a golden censer; and there was given unto him much incense, that he should add it unto the prayers of all the saints upon the golden altar which was before the throne. And the smoke of the incense, with the prayers of the saints, went up before God out of the angel's hand' (N.T. revised version).

The Bread and the Wine—Both ordinary bread and wafer bread are lawful, but in practice the latter has become general, the priest using a larger wafer than those provided for the congregation.

The wine is usually a red one, not doctored with alcohol, but pure fermented juice of the grape. There appears to be no reason why it should be red rather than white.

Reading the Gospel—When the Gospel is read below the sanctuary it symbolizes our Lord coming down to earth from heaven, the sanctuary representing heaven. Wherever the Gospel is read the congregation should stand, facing east.

Confirmation and Holy Communion—The rule is that 'none be admitted to the Holy Communion until such time as he be confirmed, or be ready and desirous to be confirmed,' but it is usual in the latter case for it to be referred to the Bishop.

The Mixed Chalice—Mixing water with wine was the general practice in the early Church, and the first Prayer Book of 1549 directed its continuance. But in the Books of 1552 and 1662 this direction does not appear. It was, however, revived in many churches during the last century. The mixing is supposed to symbolize either the union of Christ and His Church, or the union of the Godhead and the manhood in the Person of Christ, or the importance of temperance in all things, or to typify the blood and water which came from Christ's pierced side at the Crucifixion.

Fasting—Although Fasting before receiving the Holy Sacrament is not enjoined by the Church of England, it has been the custom of the Church from the earliest times.

The Collection—Alms collected during the Service are for such 'pious and charitable uses as the Minister and the Churchwardens shall think fit.' They are thus differentiated from collections at other services which are at the disposal of the Parochial Church Council. In practice, however, all collections are often lumped together in the Church accounts!

The Sermon—It is interesting to note that the only time when a sermon is ordered in the Prayer Book is during the Communion service. It is not so ordered either during Mattins or Evensong. Yet in many churches sermons are preached during these services and not during a Communion service!

Evening Communion—About the middle of the nineteenth century the practice of holding evening Communion services was started in some churches. This practice continues to-day in 'Low' Churches.

Rule as to Communicating—The Prayer Book ruling is: 'Every confirmed member of the Church shall communicate at the least three times in the year, of which Easter to be one.'

Morning Prayer and Evening Prayer

As laid down in the General Rubricks in the Prayer Book, 'all Priests and Deacons are to say daily the Morning and Evening Prayer, either privately or openly, not being let [i.e. prevented] by sickness, or some other urgent cause,' while the parish priest is also ordered to 'say the same in the parish-church or chapel where he ministereth,' provided he be not 'otherwise reasonably hindered.'

In practice to-day it is unusual, except in cathedrals and some other churches, to find the latter rule observed, whether due to neglect on the part of the clergy or non-attendance on the part of the laity.

On Sundays, however, Morning Prayer is in many churches the main (that is the best attended) service of the day.

The order for both is to be found in the Prayer Book (1662), while an alternative order was introduced in the 1928 version. It is safe to assert that in very few instances are either adhered to strictly.

Both services may be either said or sung. The lessons may be, and often are, read by lay persons. Although technically there is no provision for a sermon during either service, in each case on Sundays a sermon is generally preached. During Advent and from Septuagesima to Easter the *Benedicite*[1] replaces the *Te Deum*, and on Easter Day the Easter Anthem replaces the *Venite*.

[1] This and the following are the old Latin first words of Canticles used at Mattins.

The *Jubilate* takes the place of the *Benedictus* occasionally, but the only ruling about this is to the effect that it shall be so when the *Benedictus* 'shall happen to be read in the chapter for the day [i.e. the Second Lesson] or for the Gospel on St. John Baptist's Day.' On certain days the Athanasian Creed is ordered to be read instead of the Apostles' Creed, but this is usually ignored nowadays because of its length. In the event of either service being conducted by a Deacon or Lay Reader neither the Absolution nor the Blessing are pronounced. It is now customary for additional prayers to be read and several hymns to be sung. Morning Prayer is alternatively known as Mattins, and Evening Prayer as Evensong, and both are derived from the monastic Services of Prime and Vespers.

The Litany

The Litany is appointed to be sung or said after Morning Prayer on Sundays, Wednesdays and Fridays, and was first issued by Thomas Cranmer in 1544 for use in the processions ordered by Henry VIII when England was at war with Scotland and France.

It is usual for it to be read from a special faldstool, or Litany desk, placed in the nave of the church, just below the chancel, but it is also sung in procession in some churches on special occasions.

Baptism

The Church of England has rules and regulations which its members should, but regrettably do not always, observe.

The first rule is that of membership, brought about through the Sacrament of *Holy Baptism*, which should be administered, according to the Book of Common Prayer, 'as soon as possible after birth' and not deferred 'longer than the fourth, or at furthest the fifth, Sunday unless upon a great and reasonable cause.'

For every male-child to be baptized there must be two Godfathers and one Godmother; for every female, one Godfather and two Godmothers. The duties of Godparents are laid down in these words addressed to them by the officiating Priest:

Forasmuch as *this child hath* promised by you *his* sureties to renounce the devil and all his works, to believe in God, and to serve him; ye must remember, that it is your parts and duties to see that *this infant* be taught, so soon as he shall be able to learn, what a solemn vow, promise, and profession, *he hath* here made by you. And that *he* may know these things the better, ye shall call upon *him* to hear sermons; and chiefly ye shall provide, that *he* may learn the Creed, the Lord's Prayer, and the Ten Commandments, in the vulgar tongue, and all other things which a Christian ought to know and believe to his soul's health; and that *this child* may be virtuously brought up to lead a godly and a Christian life; remembering always, that Baptism doth represent unto us our profession; which is, to follow the example of our Saviour Christ, and to be made like unto him; that, as he died, and rose again for us, so should we, who are baptized, die from sin, and rise again unto righteousness; continually mortifying all our evil and corrupt affections, and daily proceeding in all virtue and godliness of living.

Ye are to take care that *this child* be brought to the Bishop to be Confirmed by him, so soon as *he* can say the Creed, the Lord's Prayer, and the Ten Commandments, in the vulgar tongue, and be further instructed in the Church Catechism set forth for that purpose.

In the 1928 version the wording is somewhat different, but the gist is the same.

Godparents must be baptized persons, but need not be confirmed, although in practice it is obviously desirable that they should be communicants. The parents of the child may act as Godparents provided that there be one other. In the absence of the real Godparents at a baptism others, provided they are baptized persons themselves, may act as proxies.

In the Preface to the Baptism Service it is stated that Baptism should be administered when most people come together to church, but it has long been the general procedure for Baptisms to take place semi-privately, usually in the afternoon. This has arisen partly because some parents are embarrassed when their children cry in church and partly (perhaps one should write 'chiefly') because of a lack of understanding, or appreciation, of the whole concept of the significance of the Sacrament. To this act of initiation of a Christian child of Christian parents in the presence of a Christian Church of which they are all members the element of witness is important, and it is of interest to note that there is now a tendency for Baptisms to be administered in the presence of the congregation as directed by the Prayer Book.

It is doubtful whether more than a small proportion of Godparents take their duties very seriously. Often the original presentation of a silver mug, a Premium Bond, or some other gift and the occasional 'tip' in subsequent years constitute their sole contribution towards the obligations which they originally undertook!

Infant baptism may be administered in private houses, hospitals, and other secular buildings in cases where the infant concerned is in danger of death, and in such cases when no lawful Minister can be procured and there is extreme urgency any lay member of the Church may lead the short service provided to meet such contingencies. And this is held to constitute a valid Baptism. 'Yet nevertheless, if the child, which is after this sort baptized, do afterwards live, it is expedient that it be brought into the church, to the intent that, the people being certified that it hath been duly baptized, it may be received publicly into the congregation.'

There is no fee payable for Baptism, but it is customary for a thank-offering to be made.

For those who are 'of riper years and able to answer for themselves' the special form of Baptism is set forth in the Book of Common Prayer.

All public and private Baptisms must be registered in a book provided for the purpose at the expense of the parish and kept in custody of the Incumbent in a fire-proof safe, similarly provided.

There is no age-limit for Baptism.

It is very common for 'baptism' to be called 'christening' (i.e. making a person a Christian) although the word does not occur in the service. 'Christening,' however, is also used to describe the naming of ships, bells, etc., and for many people simply means 'giving a name to' some person or thing.

Confirmation

While membership of the Church is brought about by Baptism there is a subsequent act closely associated with it, namely Confirmation.

Among the rubricks of the Order of Confirmation in the Prayer Book are these:

To the end that Confirmation may be ministered to the more edifying of such as shall receive it, the Church hath thought good to order, That none hereafter shall be confirmed, but such as can say the Creed, the Lord's Prayer, and the Ten Commandments; and can also answer to such other questions, as in the short Catechism are contained: which order is very convenient to be observed; to the end, that children, being now come to the years of discretion, and having learned what their Godfathers and Godmothers promised for them in Baptism, they may themselves, with their own mouth and consent, openly before the Church, ratify and confirm the same; and also promise, that by the grace of God they will evermore endeavour themselves faithfully to observe such things, as they, by their own confession, have assented unto.

So soon as children are come to a competent age, and can say, in their mother tongue, the Creed, the Lord's Prayer, and the Ten Commandments; and also can answer to such other questions as in the short Catechism are contained, they shall be brought to the Bishop.

The age of those baptized in infancy and subsequently confirmed varies, but in general it can be stated that it is usually between ten and fifteen, according to the mentality and disposition of the child, the views of the child's parents or guardians, and the regulations laid down by the Bishop.

The essential act of Confirmation is the laying of the Bishop's hand on the head of the person being confirmed, while he says: 'Defend, O Lord, this Thy child (or, this Thy servant) with Thy heavenly grace, that he (or she) may continue Thine for ever; and daily increase in Thy Holy Spirit more and more, until he (or she) come into Thy everlasting kingdom. Amen.'

This act may only be performed by a Bishop, and it is for this reason that Confirmations are held far less frequently than Baptisms.

It is usual for parish priests to hold Confirmation classes every year, and then to present as candidates to the Bishop those whom they consider to be suitable.

Female candidates should wear white veils on their heads. Male candidates should avoid using hair-oil for the occasion, since it is extremely unpleasant for the Bishop to lay his hand on sticky heads.

There is no age limit preventing a baptized member of the Church from being confirmed.

A priest who prepares anyone for Confirmation must, of course, ascertain when and where he, or she, was baptized.

According to the *Official Year Book of the Church of England* (1960) the number of Confirmations in 1958 was 170,735, representing 69,537 males and 101,198 females from 5,025 centres.

Matrimony

The Christian conception of marriage is that it is 'a life-long and intimate union and that anything short of this falls short of the purpose of God.'[1]

The solemnization of matrimony, according to the Rules of the Church of England, may not take place

[1] *Doctrine in the Church of England*, 1922.

until either the banns of the two persons concerned have been published, or a licence has been obtained. But it should be noted that banns and licences alike hold good for three months only and the marriage must be celebrated between 8 a.m. and 6 p.m.

The form of banns is thus:

I publish the banns of marriage between N. of the parish of ——, and N. of the parish of ——. If any of you know cause, or just impediment, why these two persons should not be joined together in Holy Matrimony, ye are to declare it. This is the first [second, or third] time of asking.

In the event of the persons residing in different parishes the banns must be read in each of them, and they must be so read on three Sundays, but not necessarily successive Sundays, preferably during a Morning Service, but if this is not possible, at an Evening one. Details must be kept in a special book and signed on each occasion by the 'publisher,' who may, incidentally, be a Lay Reader. A certificate of such banns having been properly published must be sent by the incumbent of the parish in which the marriage does not take place to the incumbent of the one in which it does.

Marriage by licence is merely a dispensation from the necessity of publishing banns. Licences are obtained by application to the Diocesan Registrar or a Surrogate (i.e. a clergyman appointed by a Diocesan Bishop as his deputy to grant licences for marriages without banns). In certain cases a special licence can be obtained from the Archbishop of Canterbury enabling a marriage to be solemnized at any convenient time or place.

No persons under the age of sixteen can be married, and in the case of persons under twenty-one the consent of parents, guardians, or a court of law must be obtained.

In general, a person over the age of sixteen has the right to be married in his parish church or in the church on the Electoral Roll of which his name has been entered.

In the case of a baptized person wishing to marry an unbaptized one the permission of the Bishop must technically be obtained, but as a rule Diocesan clergy have authority from their Bishop to marry such persons provided they are satisfied that the unbaptized party can with a good conscience and a right understanding take his or her part in the marriage service, but in the event of the unbaptized one either disclaiming faith in the Christian religion or belonging to a non-Christian religion the marriage may not be solemnized in a church.

Certain alterations in the form of service were made in the 1928 version of the Prayer Book and these are often preferred to-day. The main differences are contained in the introduction and the actual solemnization. In the old version the introduction contains the following as the causes for which Matrimony was ordained:

First, It was ordained for the procreation of children, to be brought up in the fear and nurture of the Lord, and to the praise of his holy name.

Secondly, It was ordained for a remedy against sin, and to avoid fornication; that such persons as have not the gift of continency might marry, and keep themselves undefiled members of Christ's body.

In the new version they are:

First, It was ordained for the increase of mankind according to the will of God, and that children might be brought up in the fear and nurture of the Lord, and to the praise of his holy name.

Secondly, It was ordained in order that the natural instincts and affections, implanted by God, should be hallowed and directed aright; that those who are called of God to this holy estate, should continue therein in pureness of living.

The third 'cause'—

The mutual society, help and comfort, that the one ought to have of the other, both in prosperity and adversity

is alike in both Services.

Again, the actual words of solemnization in the old version are:

Wilt thou have this woman to thy wedded wife, to live together after God's ordinance in the holy estate of Matrimony? Wilt thou love her, comfort her, honour, and keep her in sickness and in health; and, forsaking all other keep thee only unto her, so long as ye both shall live?

And,

Wilt thou have this man to thy wedded husband, to live together after God's ordinance in the holy estate of Matrimony? Wilt thou obey him, and serve him, love, honour, and keep him in sickness and in health; and, forsaking all other, keep thee only unto him, so long as ye both shall live.

Slight changes have been made. Thus in each instance for 'God's ordinance,' 'God's law' has been substituted, while in the address to the female of the party, 'Wilt thou obey him and serve him' has been altered to 'Wilt thou love him, comfort him,' etc.

Further, where in the old version the male partner says, 'I take thee, etc. . . .,' the words 'according to God's holy ordinance' are 'according to God's holy law,' and the female says, 'I take thee, etc. . . . to love, cherish, and to obey,' she says, 'to love and to cherish.'

Finally, instead of the male saying, '. . . with my body I thee worship and with all my worldly goods I thee endow,' he says, '. . . with my body I thee honour, and all my worldly goods with thee I share.'

Fees are payable for marriages.

N.B.—A marriage in a registry office is as legally valid as a marriage in church, and after the ceremony has been performed the Church makes no distinction between the two.

It is now permitted to contract a marriage with:

Deceased wife's sister,
Deceased brother's widow,
Deceased wife's brother's daughter,
Deceased wife's sister's daughter,
Father's deceased brother's widow,
Mother's deceased brother's widow,
Deceased wife's father's sister,
Deceased wife's mother's sister,
Brother's deceased son's widow,
Sister's deceased son's widow,

but no clergyman can be compelled to solemnize such a marriage.

The Burial of the Dead

The order for the Burial of the Dead is not allowed for any that die unbaptized, or for any that are excommunicated, or have knowingly committed suicide. Incidentally, it is to be noted that excommunication is a very rare occurrence in the Church of England.

The 1928 version of the Prayer Book makes some small alterations in the service, which in either version is divided into two parts, namely the service in church and the burial outside.

In the case of the body being cremated, in place of the words 'commit his (her) body to the ground, earth to earth, ashes to ashes, dust to dust,' the words 'commit his (her) body to be consumed by fire' are substituted. Similarly, at the burial of the ashes after cremation, in place of the words 'commit his (her) body to the ground, earth to earth, ashes to ashes, dust to dust,' the words 'commit his (her) ashes to the ground, earth to earth, dust to dust,' or 'commit his (her) ashes to their resting place' are used.

Unlike the Roman Catholic Church which forbids its members from disposing of their dead by means of cremation, the Church of England has not given any ruling. Accordingly the Prayer Book Order of Burial is as valid in the case of a cremated person as of an uncremated.

A resident in a parish has a right to be buried in the parish churchyard, or cemetery, irrespective of whether his name is on the electoral roll of the parish, and any person dying in a parish, or whose body is found or cast on shore from tidal or navigable waters within a parish, is regarded for the purposes of burial as a parishioner. Nevertheless this does not prevent personal representatives from removing the body and its burial taking place elsewhere.

Although parishioners have the right to be buried in the parish burial-place, they have not the right to be buried in any particular spot, this being for the incumbent to determine, unless a special Faculty has been obtained. With regard to the digging of the grave, this is the responsibility of those whose duty it is to make the funeral arrangements, and the incumbent is only responsible for pointing out the site and indicating the required depth.

There are certain fees payable for a burial, either based upon custom or fixed as part of a Table of Parochial Fees for the particular parish by the Church Commissioners or other lawful authority.

Mourning for the dead in its more ostensible forms seems to be on the decline. Those heavily crêpe-draped widows are very seldom to be seen nowadays and such things as black-edged writing paper and visiting cards have also disappeared. Nor, with the advent of motor-cars, do the black horses, adorned with black plumes, appear on the contemporary scene, while their accompanying top-hatted, black-gloved, frock-coated attendants have vanished with them. It is still, however, considered proper for a measure of black to be worn by those attending funerals, whether in the shape of a black hat for the females or a black tie for the males. Black arm-bands have gone and the change from all black to purple or grey after a definite period is no more observed. Perhaps, in the course of time, there will be a return to those early days, *c.* fourth to eighth century, when burials were an occasion of joy, and those attending wore white!

It was once customary in churches for the 'passing bell' to be rung before dark, the reason for this ancient custom being that the faithful may pray for the dying person, but the custom has largely lapsed. Nowadays a bell is often rung for some time before a funeral, but there seems to be no authority for this, since the only 'canon' concerning such tolling of bells states that '. . . after the party's death (if so it fall out) there shall be rung no more but one short peal and one other before the burial and one other after the burial.'

Commination Service

This Service, drawn up by the compilers of the Book of Common Prayer, first appeared in the Book published in 1549 and has been included in subsequent revisions.

It is designed to be used on the first day of Lent (i.e. Ash Wednesday), and at such other times 'as the ordinary shall appoint,' and is a recital of divine judgements against sinners with an exhortation to penitence and prayers.

To-day the Commination Service is seldom heard, possibly because the idea of judgement and the idea of vengeance tend to become confused and seem to deny the idea that God is a God of Love.

Churching of Women

This form of thanksgiving after childbirth has, like the Commination Service, become less frequently observed than in the past (depending somewhat on the locality).

It is intended to precede the Holy Communion, and the woman concerned is directed to 'kneel down in some convenient place, as hath been accustomed, or as the Ordinary shall direct.' Her husband shall, 'if he so desire,' accompany her. At one time a special pew was reserved in many churches for this purpose, and the woman wore a white veil. She is ordered to 'offer accustomed offerings' which are for the priest himself.

The Visitation of the Sick

The Order for the Visitation of the Sick as set forth in the Prayer Book may be used in part or in full. It is so phrased that it is apparently not intended to be used more than once during an illness and, in general, only in cases where the sick person seems likely not to recover.

There is also an office for the Communion of the Sick.

Forms of Prayer to be Used at Sea

Two prayers to be used in the Royal Navy[1] every day are included in the collection of prayers and anthems especially chosen for use at sea. Others are prayers to be used 'in storms,' 'before a fight at sea against any enemy,' 'thanksgiving after a storm,' 'thanksgiving after victory or deliverance from an enemy.' There is also a special Committal for inclusion in the Burial Service for those who are buried at sea.

Services for Children

In many churches special services designed for children are held on every Sunday. There is no authoritative set form for such services and so they vary according to the ideas of those concerned with the holding of them.

In addition, there has been of recent years an increasing number of what are called 'Children's Corners' in churches, where pictures, effigies, books, etc., of a religious nature which are thought likely to appeal to the very young are to be found.

Unction

The meaning of Unction is 'anointing with oil with a religious significance.'

In the first English Prayer Book (1549) a form of Unction was included in the Order for the Visitation of the Sick 'for use if the sick person desire.' The original purpose is recovery from sickness rather than preparation for death, but in the Middle Ages it came to be associated with imminent death, and was known as Extreme Unction. In later versions of the Prayer Book no provision for unction has been made, but in 1935 a 'Form of Unction and the Laying on of Hands' was approved by the Convocations of Canterbury and York 'for provisional use subject to due diocesan sanction.'

[1] The Royal Navy faithfully keeps this rule.

The Commission on Christian Doctrine in their report (1938) stated:

> If and when Unction is used (as to which issue we make no recommendation), it should be interpreted as an outward and visible rite, having a background both in the New Testament and in Church tradition, which, expressing the Church's pastoral care for the sick and dying, is, in the context of faith and of the Church's Ministration, a symbol of the grace of God for the strengthening of the body and soul in their weakness.

Unction is one of the traditional seven Sacraments.

Fasting

It is important to realize that fasting is not an end in itself but a means to an end, witnessing that the bodily life should be controlled by the spiritual, a guard against self-indulgence, a means of sharing in some small measure the sufferings of Christ, an expression of penitence. This is the aspect of fasting with which we are concerned here, and it has been the custom of the Church since the earliest times.

Our Lord does not appear to have instituted any fasts Himself, but His approval of the habit seems to be confirmed according to St. Luke's Gospel (v. 33–35) and St. Matthew (vi. 16–18). His insistence on its value being dependent upon the sincerity of the individual faster is to be noted.

In the Prayer Book there is a table of all the days of fasting throughout the year, which are the forty days of Lent, the Ember Days, the three Rogation Days and every Friday, except Christmas Day. A few additional times are added in the 1928 version.

Methods of fasting vary, but in general the custom of abstaining entirely from the consumption of food and drink before receiving the Holy Sacrament is observed, while many 'give up' some favourite form of food, e.g. sugar, in Lent, and there are still those who eat fish instead of meat on a Friday!

The substitution of fish for meat seems to have arisen in mediaeval times when it was considered a less desirable form of food.

The sense of the importance of fasting has certainly diminished and many reasons for this have been cited, but the fact remains that it is not only supported by ecclesiastical authority but is regarded by certain individuals as a form of self-denial which appeals to their strongest emotions.

Sunday is never regarded as a day of fasting, even in Lent. This is due to it being observed as the day on which our Lord rose from the dead and, therefore, a day for rejoicing.

Confession

There are two sorts of confession, namely public and private (or auricular).

Public confession occurs in the Holy Communion Service and in those of Morning and Evening Prayer. Private confession is confession by an individual to a priest.

This latter practice of auricular confession has always been part of the doctrine of the Church, and in the Ordering of Priests the Bishop says: 'Receive the Holy Ghost for the Office and Work of a Priest in the Church of God, now committed unto thee by the Imposition of our hands. Whose sins thou dost forgive, they are forgiven; and whose sins thou dost retain, they are retained.'

Again, the final paragraph of the first Exhortation in the Holy Communion Service is:

> Because it is requisite, that no man should come to the Holy Communion, but with a full trust in God's mercy, and with a quiet Conscience; therefore if there be any of you, who by this means cannot quiet his own conscience herein, but requireth further comfort or counsel, let him come to me, or to some other discreet and learned Minister of God's Word, and open his grief; that by the ministry of God's holy Word he may receive the benefit of absolution, together

with ghostly counsel and advice, to the quieting of his conscience, and avoiding of all scruple and doubtfulness.

The form for giving absolution after private confession is contained in the Office for the Visitation of the Sick, as follows:

Our Lord Jesus Christ, who hath left power to his Church to absolve all sinners who truly repent and believe in him, of his great mercy forgive thee thine offences: and by his authority committed to me, I absolve thee from all thy sins, In the name of the Father, and of the Son, and of the Holy Ghost. Amen.

Occasions for private confession are naturally for the individual and the confessor to arrange between them, but the Eves of the great feasts, such as Easter and Christmas, and the beginning of the long Lenten fast are regarded as especially suitable times.

The clergy are charged to keep the seal of confession with the utmost rigidity.

While private confessions are open to all members of the Church, upon none is their practice obligatory, a position which some people regard as anomalous. But it must be remembered that this does not apply to Confession both in public worship and in private prayer and the reason for the difference is due to the doctrine that there is

. . . no distinction in principle between the general confession and absolution in the public services of the Church, and the direct and individual confession and absolution for which provision is made in the Office for the Visitation of the Sick or to which reference is made in the Exhortation attached to the Order of Holy Communion. In all cases the basis of action is the Gospel itself, the proclamation of the Divine Love seeking and saving the lost and uniting them in the fellowship of the redeemed. In all cases the divine forgiveness is declared. In all cases the purpose is the bestowal of the benefit of absolution, though in one set of circumstances a special judicial element is introduced by the nature of these circumstances.[1]

[1] *Doctrine in the Church of England*, 1922.

A familiar formula summing up the Anglican position in the matter of private confession is: 'All may; none must; some ought.'

Processions

As Percy Dearmer points out in *The Parson's Handbook*, a procession 'is a distinct, significant act of worship: it is not an aimless walk round the church; but it has a definite object, such as the Rood, the Lord's Table, or the Font.'

It is, therefore, highly important that whatever shape it may take, be it large or small, elaborate or simple, it be conducted with dignity and precision. Nothing is worse, surely, than the sight of men and boys shuffling along in no sort of proper order and carrying objects askew.

In the Prayer Book (1662) the only description of a Procession is that contained in the Order for the Burial of the Dead but, nevertheless, they have been customary since ancient times.

Processions are either festal or penitential, take place only on special occasions, and in 'High' rather than in 'Low' Churches.

The ancient order for a Eucharistic procession was as follows: The vergers, with their wands, making way for the procession, the boy with holy water (in surplice), the 'acolitus,' or clerk, carrying the Cross, the two torch-bearers, the thurifer, the sub-deacon, the deacon, the celebrant, the boys of the choir, the men of the choir, other clergy. If a bishop is present he walks last of all, unless he is to officiate, when he takes the place of the celebrant.

Creeds

The three Creeds contained in the Book of Common Prayer are the Apostles', the Nicene, and the Athanasian.

They are all affirmations of faith. As Archbishop William Temple has written:

> The function of the creed is not to be itself an object of faith, but to point man to what is worthy to be accepted as an object of faith, and it is in that proper object of faith, and not in the creed, that true spiritual authority is to be found.

The *Apostles' Creed* was first so called in the fourth century, when in form, though not in exactly the same words, it approximated to the creed as we know it to-day and as it has been known since the eighth century. By the early part of the Middle Ages it was used at Baptisms and the practice of reciting it at daily services began soon afterwards.

It forms part of the Order for Morning and Evening Prayer, except on thirteen days when the Athanasian Creed should take its place, but as this latter regulation has been almost universally ignored for a long time, (presumably because of its great length), the Apostles' Creed is recited on those thirteen days also. In the 1928 version of the Prayer Book the Athanasian Creed is no longer 'ordered,' but the priest is advised that he 'may' sing or say it on certain days! The Apostles' Creed also forms part of the Service of Holy Baptism, the Catechism and Compline (1928 Prayer Book).

The *Nicene Creed* originated from the first Council of Nicaea (325) but was somewhat shorter than the creed generally known by that name. It ran:

> We believe in one God, the Almighty Father, creator of all things visible and invisible. And in one Lord Jesus Christ, the Son of God, who alone was begotten of the Father, God of God, Light of Light, through whom all was made that was in heaven and on earth, who for us men and for our salvation came down and became flesh, became man, suffered and rose on the third day, is ascended to heaven and will come to judge the living and the dead. And in the Holy Spirit.

The Nicene Creed, included in the Prayer Book, contains various additions, and is of a later date. It was first recited at the Eucharist in the East in the fifth century and gradually spread to the West. In the early Middle Ages the 'Filioque' was added to the section about the Holy Spirit ('who proceedeth from the Father *and the Son*').

The *Athanasian Creed* is seldom said or sung in our churches to-day and, indeed, efforts have been made from time to time to have it removed altogether from the Prayer Book. Its object is to expound, firstly, the doctrine of the Trinity and, secondly, the doctrine of the Incarnation. The 1928 Prayer Book contains a revised translation of it, but the great majority of people find it extremely difficult to understand. It was composed during the early part of the fifth century.

THE BIBLE

The two versions of the Bible in use are the Authorized of 1611 and the Revised of 1881–85, the former greatly predominating over the latter. In fact, neither of them has ever been officially 'ordered' to be read, that distinction being confined to the Great Bible of 1539. Following the Great Bible came first the Geneva Bible (1560) and then the Bishops' Bible (1568). There are also various comparatively recent translations, such as the American Revised Standard Version, the Bible designed to be read as Literature, the New English Bible, etc.

It is the text-book of the Church, but there are many passages in it which are difficult to understand both in the Old and the New Testaments. Although commonly referred to as 'The Bible,' it should rightly be called 'The Holy Bible,' since the word 'Bible' is simply the English equivalent of the Greek word 'biblia,' meaning 'books.'

For many centuries the contents of the Bible were accepted by the faithful as being literally true, but as the years went by this traditional view was increasingly questioned, and at the end of the last century both literary and historical criticism was applied to both the Old and New Testaments mainly by Christian scholars, with the result that many of the erstwhile beliefs were abandoned. As Dr. Garbett, Archbishop of York, has written:[1]

> Much of the perplexity caused by the new views on the Bible, as they reached the man in the street, or even the man in the pew, was due to past failure to give intelligent teaching. The fear the clergy felt of disturbing the faithful by plain statements led many of their congregations to be caught unawares by Biblical criticism, and in violent reaction from the traditional views they rejected the Bible as the Word of God. They discovered that the description of the creation in Genesis is not a scientific account of the origin of life, that the world was not covered with a flood, that a great fish did not swallow Jonah, and therefore hastily concluded that most of the Bible is unworthy of belief.
>
> In spite, however, of the fact that there are many passages in the Bible which cannot be accepted as literally true and that all parts do not stand on one spiritual level, it remains, and must remain, the text-book of the Church, an inspired record of a unique revelation, its theme God speaking to men, the chief source of guidance for a Christian life, and the final criterion of Anglican doctrine.

The Apocrypha

This is the name given to those books included in the Septuagint and Vulgate versions of the Old Testament, not originally written in Hebrew and not counted as genuine by the Jews, and which were excluded from the Sacred Canon after the Reformation by Protestant leaders on the grounds that they were not inspired. The Church of England uses them in her public Offices, and reads them for example and instruction but not as the basis for doctrine.

Breeches Bible

This is a popular name for the Geneva Bible of 1560 and so called because of the translation of Genesis iii. 7,

[1] *In an Age of Revolution*, by Cyril Garbett, D.D.

where 'breeches' is the word used for the 'aprons' (A.V.) of fig-leaves made by Adam and Eve.

The Book of Common Prayer

Generally known as the 'Prayer Book,' this is the Official Service book of the Church of England and contains the forms for administration of the Sacraments and other public and private rites as well as the daily Offices of Morning and Evening Prayer, the Psalms and the Ordinal.

It was originally compiled, largely by Thomas Cranmer, in order to simplify and condense, in English, the Latin services of the Mediaeval Church, and in 1549 the 'First Prayer Book of Edward VI' was printed and enforced as the National Use by the first Act of Uniformity.

This book was revised in 1552 as the 'Second Prayer Book of Edward VI,' but before it came into general use the Act of Repeal under Queen Mary restored the ancient Latin services. However, in 1559, after Queen Elizabeth had succeeded to the throne, it was re-issued with slight alterations and remained unchanged until the end of the sixteenth century. On the accession of James I, the Puritans, who had been objecting for some time to certain portions of the Book, put forward a petition to the King. This, amongst many other factors, led to a final revision published in 1662, and this is the Book of Common Prayer in general use to-day.

There is also what is known as the 1928 Book which was passed in both Convocations as well as the Church Assembly, but rejected by Parliament. Its use, subject to the Bishop's consent, is nevertheless quite frequent and usually approved by the congregation. Its object is to make the Services more intelligible by shortening them, simplifying the language, and providing additional prayers.

It may be of interest to recall what took place in

connection with the attempt to obtain the Royal Assent to its use. In short, the situation developed in this way:

In 1927 a Draft Book was presented to the Convocations and to the Church Assembly and passed by large majorities, that of the Church Assembly being 517 to 13 (the Bishops voting as to 34 in favour and 4 against). A Resolution under the Church of England Assembly (Powers) Act, 1919, directing that the Measure should be presented to His Majesty was subsequently passed by 241 votes to 88 in the House of Lords, but was rejected in the House of Commons by 238 to 205 votes. Early in the following year (1928) a second Measure (known as the Prayer Book Measure, 1928) was introduced in the Church Assembly, went through the same procedure as before, securing majorities in the Convocations and the Church Assembly, but was rejected by the House of Commons (226 votes to 220).

The privilege of printing the Book of Common Prayer is confined to the Queen's Printer and the University Presses of Oxford and Cambridge, to which an Order in Council from the Privy Council Office is transmitted on the occasion of any necessary change (e.g. of names in the State prayers).

Hymn Books

There is no official hymn book in the Church of England.

Those in general use are *Hymns, Ancient and Modern*, of which there are two editions, and the *English Hymnal*, published in 1906, and revised in 1933. The latter is, perhaps, more frequently found in Anglo-Catholic Churches than the former, but there is no general rule.

There is also *Songs of Praise*, published in 1925 and revised in 1931, but this is not nearly so often used as *Ancient and Modern* and the *English Hymnal*.

The older books, such as *Church Hymns*, seem to have entirely disappeared.

The choice of hymn books rests with the Incumbent.

Rubrics

Rubrics are the directions printed at the beginning of service books or in the course of the text. In mediaeval books they were written in red so as to distinguish them from the text of the services. Hence the term 'rubric' (Lat.: *ruber:* red). The rubric in the Book of Common Prayer which has given and continues to give rise to most controversy is known as the 'Ornaments rubric' which was inserted in the 1559 edition and states that the ornaments of the Church and of the Ministers thereof should be those in use 'by the authority of Parliament, in the second year of the reign of King Edward VI.'

The trouble over this arises from the fact that it refers back to a certain period, but does not give a detailed list of the ornaments and vestments to be used.

The *Black Rubric* is the name given to the 'Declaration on kneeling' printed at the end of the Holy Communion Service in the Book of Common Prayer, the reason being that it was printed in black in the nineteenth century when the custom of *printing* the rubrics in red was introduced. In recent times the rubrics have been generally all printed in black, but, where the two-colour system is maintained, the black rubric is now printed in red.

The Lessons

Two portions of the Bible, one from the Old Testament and the other from the New, are appointed to be read at Morning and Evening Prayer. The Kalendar (of 1871) contained in the Prayer Book is now seldom, if ever, adhered to, and it is usual to have resource to the Lectionary of 1922, revised in 1928, and several times since.

Lessons may be read by the laity, the reader being

ordered to begin and end the lessons with the words: 'Here beginneth such a chapter, or verse of such a chapter, of such a book,' and 'Here endeth the first (or second) lesson.' But customs tend to vary and the New Lectionary provides a different form of words.

In some churches to-day the reader delivers a brief description of the contents of the lessons before reading them, and, while there is no authority for so doing, the custom would seem to be helpful to many listeners.

Special lessons are appointed for certain days.

Liturgical Colours

Although the custom of using different colours according to the seasons in the Church's year came into being early in the Middle Ages, it was not until later that there was an ordered sequence in the Western Church.

That which is in common use to-day is known as the Exeter sequence, and is as follows:

Advent	— violet, purple or blue
Christmas	— white
Epiphany	— white
Epiphany octave to Septuagesima	— green
Septuagesima to Good Friday	— violet, purple or blue
Eastertide	— white
Rogations	— violet, purple or blue
Ascensiontide	— white
Whitsuntide	— red
Trinity	— white
Trinity to Advent	— green
Anniversary or Consecration of a church	— white
Festival of patron saint of a church	— colour of the Saint's Day
An Apostle, Evangelist or Martyr	— red
Confessor	— green or yellow
A Virgin	— white
Virgin who is also a Martyr	— red and white

Baptisms and Confirmations	— white
Marriages, Churching of Women, Thanksgivings	— white
Harvest Festivals	— white
Visitation and Communion of the Sick	— violet
Commination Service	— violet
Burial of Dead and Requiems	— violet or black

The Catechism

The definition of the word 'Catechism' is 'Instruction by question and answer' and it may be applied to various matters, but commonly the word refers to the Prayer Book catechism which is 'to be learned of every person before he be brought to be confirmed by the Bishop.'

It is in two parts: (1) the baptismal covenant, the Creed, the Ten Commandments, and the Lord's Prayer; (2) the meaning of the two Sacraments of Baptism and Holy Communion.

The first part was composed and modified between 1549 and 1661: the second was written in 1604.

According to the rubrics of the Prayer Book the clergy are enjoined to teach the catechism 'upon Sundays and Holy Days after the second lesson in Evening Prayer' but this custom has long fallen into disuse. Instead it is usual for such teaching to be given in Sunday Schools, or at special services for children in church on Sunday afternoons, or in the evenings when confirmation classes are often held.

Sermons

The Sermon is ordered in the Prayer Book to be preached at the Communion Service, but in the majority of churches it is preached at Mattins and/or Evensong.

There was a great vogue for sermons in Elizabethan and Jacobean times, particularly among the Puritans, who combined religious instruction with political intrigue. Men like Barrow, Stillingfleet and, above all, Tillotson in the later period were fine preachers. Sermons were long, lasting perhaps an hour or even longer.

In the Elizabethan period, according to G. M. Trevelyan,[1]

> Weekly attendance at church was a duty enforced by the State. There was a statutory fine on absentees. . . . A Catholic gentleman of Cornwall, John Trevelyan, who used to attend church to avoid the fine, endured the reading of the lesson and the singing of the 'Geneva Jig' which was his name for Sternhold and Hopkins' psalms, but always went out before the sermon, calling aloud to the parson in the pulpit, 'when thou hast said what thou hast to say, come and dine with me.'

By those clergy whose educational standard was not very high readings from the Books of Homilies often took the place of a sermon.

The power of the pulpit seems to have declined with the passing of time. The increase in the number of books published, the daily and weekly press and, of more modern growth, broadcasting and television have all contributed to this decline, while the diminishing numbers in the average church congregation has been another factor.

Writing to a friend in 1930 Bishop Hensley Henson lays bare some interesting and amusing details concerning suitable rules for a preacher to adopt when preaching before His Majesty King George V, viz.:

1. Do not, at most, exceed 15 minutes.
2. Take no notice at all of His Majesty but just preach quite naturally as if it were an ordinary congregation which you were addressing.
3. Avoid 'high falutin' and be straightforward and simple.
4. Speak up clearly because His Majesty is getting a little deaf.
5. It would be quite fitting and would probably be appreciated, if you said something at firsthand about miners' lives. The King is much interested in social questions.

[1] *English Social History.*

The liking for short sermons may have been inherited from his grandmother, Queen Victoria, who had the same preference and was accustomed to let it be known that the limit of her endurance was likely to be reached shortly after ten minutes—a time limit which was, one understands, only extended in the case of the Rt. Rev. W. Boyd Carpenter, Bishop of Ripon, a preacher of outstanding eloquence and a prelate of whom she was especially fond!

The most famous sermon is, of course, the Sermon on the Mount.

Consecration

By consecration is meant the separation of a thing or person for sacred functions. The consecrating of the bread and wine at the service of Holy Communion is an example. Others are the consecration of Bishops by the laying on of hands by other Bishops, the consecration of a church by a Bishop and of altars and Eucharistic vessels within a church.

Anthems

Anthems are scriptural words set to vocal music and sung by the choir alone. They may be for solo voices only, for a full choir or for a mixture of both and are sung after the third collect at Morning or Evening Prayer instead of a hymn. In the Book of Common Prayer the direction is: 'In Quires and Places where they sing, here followeth the Anthem,' with no mention of hymns, but in the average church they occur only occasionally. During the singing of an anthem the congregation should be seated.

Feasts and Holy Days

Easter Day is always the first Sunday after the full moon which happens upon or next after the twenty-first day of March, and if the full moon happens upon a Sunday, Easter Day is the next Sunday.

Septuagesima Sunday is nine weeks before Easter.

Sexagesima Sunday is eight weeks before Easter.

Quinquagesima Sunday is seven weeks before Easter.

Ash Wednesday is in the week following Quinquagesima Sunday and is the beginning of *Lent*, which ends on Easter Eve.

Rogation Sunday is five weeks after Easter Day, and the *Rogation Days* are the three following days.

Ascension Day is forty days after Easter Day.

Whitsunday is seven weeks after Easter Day.

Trinity Sunday is the Sunday following Whit Sunday.

Advent Sunday is always the Sunday nearest to the Feast of St. Andrew (November 30th), whether before, or after, or the day of the Feast itself.

The Ember Days at the four seasons are the Wednesday, Friday and Saturday after: The First Sunday in Lent; The Feast of Pentecost; September 14th; December 13th.

THE GREATER FEASTS

All Sundays in the year.

January	1st	— The Circumcision of our Lord
,,	6th	— The Epiphany
,,	25th	— The Conversion of St. Paul
February	2nd	— The Purification of the Blessed Virgin
,,	24th	— St. Matthias, Apostle
March	25th	— The Annunciation of the Blessed Virgin
April	25th	— St. Mark the Evangelist
May	1st	— St. Philip and St. James, Apostles
		— The Ascension of our Lord
June	11th	— St. Barnabas, Apostle
,,	24th	— The Nativity of St. John Baptist
,,	29th	— St. Peter, Apostle
July	22nd	— St. Mary Magdalene
,,	25th	— St. James, Apostle

August	6th	—	The Transfiguration of our Lord
„	24th	—	St. Bartholomew, Apostle
September	21st	—	St. Matthew, Apostle
„	29th	—	St. Michael and All Angels
October	18th	—	St. Luke, Apostle
„	28th	—	St. Simon and St. Jude, Apostles
November	1st	—	All Saints
„	30th	—	St. Andrew, Apostle
December	21st	—	St. Thomas, Apostle
„	25th	—	The Nativity of our Lord (Christmas Day)
„	26th	—	St. Stephen, Martyr
„	27th	—	St. John the Evangelist
„	28th	—	Holy Innocents

Note on the Church's Seasons

Advent: The time of preparation for the coming of our Lord and also the beginning of the Church's year.

Christmas: The birth of our Lord.

Epiphany: The manifestion of our Lord to the Gentiles.

Lent: The Commemoration of our Lord's forty days in the wilderness (beginning on Ash Wednesday and ending on Easter Even).

Easter: The festival of our Lord's Resurrection.

Ascension: The withdrawal of our Lord into heaven.

Whitsun: The celebration of the descent of the Holy Spirit upon the Apostles.

Trinity: The union of the Three Persons (Father, Son, Holy Spirit) in one Godhead.

Mothering Sunday

Mothering Sunday is the name often given to the fourth Sunday in Lent, which is also known as Refreshment Sunday.

The name 'Mothering' probably originated from the habit of families visiting 'Mother Church' on that day, presumably on account of the reference (in the Epistle) to Jerusalem 'the mother of us all.' There also seems to have arisen a custom of visiting one's mother and presenting her with a gift, taking at one time the form of a cake, called a 'simnel,' a rich sort of plum-pudding.

The custom lapsed for a time but seems recently to have been revived, much to the advantage of florists who do a roaring trade selling the flowers which are now the usual form of gift to mothers.

Ember Days

Four seasons of three days each, observed as days of fasting and of special prayer for those about to be ordained, are known as Ember Days, and occur on the Wednesdays, Fridays and Saturdays in the weeks following Holy Cross Day (Sept. 14th), St. Lucy's Day (Dec. 13th), the first Sunday in Lent, and Whitsunday. The days of ordination are the Sundays following the Ember Days.

Rogation Days

These are the three days preceding the Ascension Day, the previous Sunday being commonly called Rogation Sunday.

They are days prescribed for prayer and fasting and for intercession for God's blessing on the fruits of the earth.

Before the Reformation, Rogation processions with the singing of litanies through the fields were usual, but these were suppressed and in place of them, under Queen Elizabeth, perambulation of each parish was ordered.

The ancient custom has to some extent been revived in more recent times and Rogation services held in the open country are not infrequent to-day.

Decalogue

This is the name given to the Ten Commandments revealed to Moses on Mount Sinai and engraven on two tablets of stone. The word is derived from two Greek words, i.e. *deka*, meaning 'ten,' and *logos*, meaning 'word.'

Carols

In earlier days the singing of carols was associated with dancing and with different seasons of the Church's year, but in more modern times this custom has lapsed and to-day they are as a rule sung only at Christmas.

They were usually sung in the open air, as they often are to-day. Shakespeare, in *A Midsummer Night's Dream*, writes 'No night is now with hymn or carol blest' and some of fifteenth-century date have been handed down, and are contained in the *Oxford Book of Carols* (1928).

The singing of carols in churches is, as in the case of hymns, from custom and not authority. They are essentially songs of joy.

Cribs

The Christmas Crib is a representation of the Manger in which the Child Jesus was laid at His birth and is often to be seen now in churches, where it is placed on Christmas Eve and where it remains until the Octave of the Epiphany (Jan. 13th). Figures of the Blessed Virgin Mary, St. Joseph, cattle, angels and shepherds are included and, of course, that of the Holy Child Himself.

Acts of Reverence

Various acts of reverence have been customary among churchgoers from the earliest times. To take the most common example, there is the custom for males to remove head-dress whilst inside a church, whether a service be in progress or not. (But it is to be noted that the equally common example of females *wearing* some form of head-dress has to some extent lapsed!)

Other examples are:

1. Bowing towards the altar on entering and leaving a church.
2. Bowing at the name of 'Jesus.'
3. Bowing during the *Gloria*.
4. Bowing at the words 'Holy, Holy, Holy' in the *Te Deum*.
5. Bowing, or kneeling, at the *Incarnatus* in the Nicene Creed.
6. Turning towards the East during the Creeds and the *Gloria*. (But as in most churches the congregation are facing East already this practice is automatically performed.)
7. Making the sign of the Cross.
8. Standing during certain parts of the service, and kneeling during others.

Concerning such acts of reverence the Book of Common Prayer gives but few directions, except with regard to standing and kneeling. The habit of half-sitting, half-crouching, while no doubt beneficial for the creases of trousers and the 'hang' of skirts, is not recognized as a proper position for members of the congregation to adopt at any time! Naturally, in the case of those who for some physical reason are unable to kneel, the directions do not apply and to receive the Holy Sacrament either standing or sitting for this reason does not, of course, invalidate its reception in any way.

Thirty-nine Articles

The Thirty-nine Articles of Religion as set forth at the end of the Book of Common Prayer were first given legal sanction in the year 1571.

There are a series of doctrinal statements to which all clergymen have to subscribe before being ordained; but this is intended to represent a general assent and not a detailed adherence to all the statements in the Articles, some of which are expressed in terminology of the sixteenth century now out-worn. What, in fact, they are assenting to is that the Articles are agreeable to the Word of God and that they will not teach in contradiction to them. The laity are not required to subscribe to them. On the first occasion of an incumbent officiating in a new parish he recites these Thirty-nine Articles. This is known as 'reading himself in,' and is probably the only occasion when most members of the congregation become aware of the contents of the Articles.

Versicles and Responses

Short sentences recited by priest and people alternately.

Canticles

Songs taken from the Bible and used in liturgical worship: *Benedictus*, *Magnificat*, *Nunc Dimittis*, *Benedicite*.

By custom, the *Te Deum*, Athanasian Creed, *Jubilate*, *Cantate*, etc., are also termed 'canticles.'

The book in the Bible called the Song of Solomon is also known as Canticles.

Prime and Compline

In the 1928 version of the Prayer Book an Order for Prime and an Order for Compline are included.

Prime is designed to be said 'at any convenient time before or after the saying of Morning Prayer, but not in substitution therefor.' It is derived from the Office appointed for the first hour, i.e. 6 a.m., in the Rule of St. Benedict.

Compline (pronounced 'Complin') is designed to be used 'when Evensong has been previously said.' Like Prime it is derived from the Rule of St. Benedict.

Harvest Thanksgiving

Although Harvest Thanksgiving Services, sometimes called Harvest Festivals, are held in most churches, and in some—especially in rural districts—are the best attended of any, they are unofficial. However, owing to their increasing popularity the Convocation of Canterbury issued in 1862 a form of service and the proposed Prayer Book of 1928 included a special collect to follow that of the day and also a special Epistle[1] and Gospel.[2]

It is generally agreed that it was the Rev. R. S. Hawker, the rather eccentric Vicar of Morwenstow, in Cornwall, who, in 1843, introduced harvest festivals into the modern English Church, thus reviving the custom of the mediaeval Church of solemnly blessing at Mass bread made from the first-fruits of the harvest.

It is customary for the church to be decorated with fruit, vegetables and flowers, which are subsequently sold and the proceeds given to some charity, and the giant marrows which often appear on these occasions have become legendary!

Intercessions

Intercessory prayer means prayer for others, and forms a very important part of the Christian practice of prayer, backed by the belief that such prayer certainly helps those on whose behalf it is offered.

Red Letter Days

These are the days of feasts or saints' days for which a proper Collect, Epistle and Gospel are provided in the Prayer Book. They are so described because they were at one time printed in ecclesiastical kalendars in red.

Vigil

The name given to the eve of the following feasts: The Nativity of our Lord; The Purification of the Blessed Virgin Mary; The Annunciation of the Blessed Virgin Mary; Easter Day; Ascension Day; Pentecost; St. Matthias; St. John Baptist; St. Peter; St. James; St.

[1] Galatians vi. 6–10. [2] St. John iv. 31–36.

Bartholomew; St. Matthew; St. Simon and St. Jude; St. Andrew; St. Thomas; All Saints' Day.

If any of these feast days fall upon a Monday, then the Vigil or Fast Day is kept on the Saturday and not upon the Sunday next before it.

When a feast has a vigil the custom is for the special Collect appointed for the feast to be said at the previous evening service. The only vigil for which a special Collect, Epistle and Gospel are appointed is Easter Even.

The Accession Service

The Prayer Book contains special forms of Morning and Evening Prayer (with proper psalms, lessons, etc.) 'for use in all churches and chapels upon the Anniversary of the Day of the Accession of the reigning Sovereign, or upon such other Day as shall be appointed by Authority.'

There are also a proper Collect, Epistle and Gospel at the Eucharist, and a separate service which 'may also be used on the same day at any convenient time.' This begins with the *Te Deum* which is followed by prayers and responses.

At the beginning of each reign a fresh Order in Council concerning the service is issued. At present the use of the service has been ordered only for churches in the provinces of Canterbury and York.

Some Statistics

According to *The Official Year Book of the Church of England* (1960) the number of those who were ordained deacons during 1959 was 512, the number of confirmations during 1958 was 170,735.

It is interesting to note that in 1931 when 498 deacons were ordained, the population, according to the most recent census, was 37,510,817, while in 1959 there were only fourteen more, although the population, according to the 1951 census, was some four million greater.

With regard to Easter communicants the following details are given in *The Church of England* (Mayfield, 1958):

Year	*Easter Communicants*	*Population*	*Percentage to Population*
1920	2,171,619	35,197,498	6.2
1930	2,301,635	37,314,946	6.4
1940	2,134,897	39,355,279	5.4
1950	1,995,573	41,138,702	4.8

According to the author, Archdeacon Mayfield, the decline ended in 1950, and three years later the number of Easter communicants was 2,068,829, and the number of confirmations which was 139,431 in 1951 had increased to 162,848 in 1955.

The latest figures for Easter communicants (1958) give 2,248,229.

Statistics, it has been said, can be made to prove anything, but, nevertheless, there does appear to be some increase in the number of those whose membership of the Church is both real and apparent!

It is also interesting to note, in view of the Church of Rome's much publicized 'conversions,' that in the period 1954–56, 10,440 Roman Catholics joined the Church of England. During the same period, 33,884 persons from other religious persuasions also joined the Church.[1]

Alms and Oblations

The word 'alms' means money collected in church whether during a service or through a box permanently placed near the doors.

The word 'oblations' is the term applied to the bread and wine offered for consecration in the Holy Communion and to any other gift, such as fruit, altar cloths, etc., presented for the use of the clergy, the sick, the poor, the church, etc.

[1] 'Conversions' in 1958 were 3,771 Roman Catholics and 6,959 of other persuasions.

When money is collected during a church service it is usually called the offertory or the collection. Technically, the word offertory should be used solely in connection with the Holy Communion, and it applies to that section of the Service which begins after the saying of the Creed and ends with the Absolution.

Reservation

This is the name given to the practice of keeping the elements, consecrated at the Eucharist. It is a very controversial question and only in a comparatively few churches is the practice observed. Where it is so, a light will be found burning in the near neighbourhood of the place where the Sacrament is preserved.

The Report of the Commission on Christian Doctrine (1922) states:

> The members of the Commission are agreed that the use of the reserved Sacrament is a 'valid' means of giving sacramental communion; they are agreed also that the extent to which and the circumstances in which this method should be employed may properly be determined by any particular Church. The decision on these questions involves, however, a variety of practical considerations (e.g. what will best tend to edification, will best serve the Communion of the Sick, and will best promote a right attitude and sound beliefs as to the Eucharist) and we hold it to be outside the province of the Commissioners, here as elsewhere, to express an opinion on administrative or pastoral questions.

Coronations

The pomp and pageantry associated with the coronation of Sovereigns is apt to disguise from the uninitiated the truc sacramental nature of the occasion. The rite falls into three parts, viz. (1) the Oath made by the Sovereign; (2) the Consecration and Anointing; (3) the Vesting, Crowning and Enthronement followed by the Homage and Holy Communion.

It has always been the privilege of the Archbishop of

Canterbury to perform the chief acts, and, in the event of there being a Queen Consort, it is his privilege to crown her also. It is true that in the case of King Edward VII and Queen Alexandra, the Archbishop of Canterbury crowned the former and the Archbishop of York the latter, but this was due to the age and infirmity of the Archbishop of Canterbury. Only on two occasions has the Archbishop of Canterbury failed to take the leading part. One was when both William I and his Consort were crowned by the Archbishop of York, and the other was when Edward II and his Consort were both crowned by the Bishop of Winchester, acting under Commission from the Archbishop who was abroad.

Various changes have occurred in the service as the centuries have passed, but the main parts have remained constant. The first time that English was used, instead of Latin, was at the Coronation of James I, and in the particular instance of James II, who was a Roman Catholic, considerable alterations were made. Among other changes made from time to time may be mentioned the omission of the sermon, the singing of the litany in procession, the transference of the singing of the *Te Deum* to the Recess, the abbreviation of the Homage to the senior member only of each rank, and certain alterations in the Oath.

The Anointing is done on the palms of both the Sovereign's hands, on the breast, and on the crown of the head, the Archbishop saying: 'Be thy hands anointed with holy oil; be thy breast anointed with holy oil; be thy head anointed with holy oil, as kings, priests and prophets were anointed: and as Solomon was anointed king by Zadok the priest and Nathan the prophet, so be you anointed, blessed and consecrated King over the Peoples, whom the Lord your God hath given you to rule and govern, In the Name of the Father, and of the Son, and of the Holy Ghost. Amen.'

The crowning is accompanied by the words: 'God crown you with a crown of glory and righteousness, that by the ministry of this our benediction, having a right faith and manifold fruit of good works, you may obtain the crown of an everlasting kingdom by the gift of Him Whose kingdom endureth for ever. Amen.'

After the crowning comes the presentation to the Sovereign of a copy of the Holy Bible: 'Our gracious King; we present you with this Book, the most valuable thing that this world affords. Here is wisdom; this is the royal Law; these are the lively Oracles of God.'

There follows the Benediction: 'The Lord bless you and keep you: and as He hath made you King over His people, so may He prosper you in this world, and make you partake of His eternal felicity in the world to come. Amen.'

'The Lord give you fruitful lands and healthful seasons; victorious fleets and armies, and a quiet Empire; a faithful Senate, wise and upright counsellors and magistrates, a loyal nobility, and a dutiful gentry; a pious and learned and useful clergy; an honest, peaceable and obedient commonalty. Amen.'

Finally, the enthronement and the Archbishop's words: 'Stand firm, and hold fast from henceforth the seat and state of royal and imperial dignity, which is this day delivered unto you, in the Name and by the authority of Almighty God, and by the hands of us the Bishops and servants of God, though unworthy: and as you see us to approach nearer to God's Altar, so vouchsafe the more graciously to continue to us your royal favour and protection. And the Lord God Almighty, Whose ministers we are, and the stewards of His mysteries, establish your Throne in righteousness, that it may stand fast for evermore, like as the sun before him, and as the faithful witness in heaven. Amen.'

After the Homage which the Archbishop, on behalf of himself and his brother Bishops, is the first to do, the Coronation of the Queen takes place, and then the Holy Communion Service follows, their Majesties' oblations having been first placed on the altar. Only the Archbishops, the Dean of Westminster, the assistant Bishops (i.e. those who have read the Epistle and the Gospel) and the Sovereign and his Consort receive the Sacrament.

From this abbreviated account of the Coronation Service it will be seen that the whole ceremony takes place within the framework of the Holy Communion, and thus its Sacramental nature is emphasized.

CHAPTER FIVE

CHURCH BUILDINGS

CATHEDRALS

THE cathedral church is the mother church of a diocese and contains the Bishop's official seat, or throne (*cathedra*), which is usually set on the north side of the Sanctuary.

The majority of cathedrals in England are of outstanding size and grandeur, and are situated in cities or towns. Before the Reformation they were divided into 'monastic' and 'secular' cathedrals according to the type of clergy attached to them. Thus when these formed a monastic establishment, bound by certain vows, they were 'monastic,' but when they were a college of clergy governed by a code of statutes or canons they were 'secular.'

The secular cathedrals of the 'Old Foundation' were Chichester, Exeter, Hereford, Lichfield, Lincoln, St. Paul's (London), Salisbury, Wells and York. The monastic cathedrals were Bath, Canterbury, Carlisle, Coventry, Durham, Ely, Norwich, Rochester, Winchester, Worcester. All these monastic cathedrals except Carlisle, which was a Church of Augustinians, were Benedictine.

After the Reformation Henry VIII founded the following: Bristol, Chester, Gloucester, Oxford and Peterborough. Modern cathedrals, i.e. since 1836, are Birmingham, Blackburn, Bradford, Bury St. Edmunds, Chelmsford, Coventry, Derby, Guildford, Leicester, Liverpool, Manchester, Newcastle, Portsmouth, Ripon, St. Albans, Sheffield, Southwark, Southwell, Truro and Wakefield.

The seats of the Diocesan Bishops have not always been in the same places, e.g. Selsey moved to Chichester, Sherborne to Salisbury, Lichfield to Chester (Lichfield, however, was subsequently refounded). Occasionally there have been two churches each containing a throne for the Bishop in a Diocese, e.g. Bath and Wells, Lichfield and Coventry. The name Bath and Wells still remains, but Lichfield and Coventry are now separate dioceses. In the case of Bath and Wells the Cathedral Church is at Wells and the abbey-church at Bath serves as a parish church.

The constitution of the body of clergy attached to a cathedral is outlined in the Chapter on Church Administration (*vide* p. 25).

Attached to some of the cathedrals are schools, many of which are of extremely ancient foundation, that at York having been founded in the seventh century. They were established for the education of the choirboys, but most of them have in later times taken fee-paying pupils, both day boys and boarders.

The increasing interest taken by the laity in the cathedrals in modern times was given prominence in 1927 when Dr. G. K. A. Bell, then Dean, initiated the Society of the Friends of Canterbury Cathedral. Since then various other such societies in connection with other cathedrals have been formed. Immense sums of money, too, have been and are being subscribed in order to restore these ancient buildings, many of which have deteriorated grievously with the passing of the centuries. New ones, such as Guildford and Liverpool, have been built and that at Coventry re-built.

Abbeys

The definition of an abbey is: 'buildings occupied by monks or nuns under an abbot or abbess; a church or house that was once an abbey or part of it.'

So far as the first part of this definition applies there are not many abbeys in England. Nashdom at Burnham, in Buckinghamshire, where a community of priests and laymen live under the rule of St. Benedict, is one, and there is another belonging to the same community at

Alton, in Hampshire. There are also a few housing communities of women devoted to the religious life, such as Laleham, near Staines in Middlesex, belonging to the Sisters of St. Peter the Apostle; Burnham, near Maidenhead, where the Society of the Precious Blood has a community; and St. Mary's at West Malling, in Kent, which is Benedictine. Most of the others are called convents, mission houses or by some other name.

With regard to the second part of the definition, the outstanding example is Westminster Abbey which is unique among English churches. Here, before the Norman Conquest, was a great Benedictine Monastery of which it was the Abbey Church. The monastery was dissolved during the Reformation in 1540, but the church remained and became more and more a great national shrine. It was, and remains, independent of the Diocese of London, and is a 'Royal Peculiar,' coming directly under the personal jurisdiction of the Sovereign, whose coronation takes place within its walls. On occasions of great national importance Westminster Abbey is the site of suitable celebrations and it is traditionally the burial place of famous men.

English abbeys in the past belonged exclusively to the following monastic orders: Benedictines, Cistercians, Premonstratensians and Augustinians.

There are several other churches which retain the name of 'Abbey,' such as Bath, Tewkesbury, Sherborne, Dorchester, etc., and they are now parish churches. Also there are the ruins of many famous abbeys of the past, e.g. Fountains, Glastonbury, Bayham, Rievaulx, Easby and others.

Priories

A priory is a religious house presided over by a prior or prioress. There are a few churches in England still called by the name of Priory since originally they formed part of one, e.g. Lanercost in Cumberland. They are now parish churches or buildings housing Anglican religious communities.

Minsters

Originally the meaning of 'minster' was a monastic establishment, or its church, but it has also been given to certain Cathedrals, such as York, and to other large churches, such as Wimborne. It has no particular significance to-day.

Parish Churches

By Parish Church is meant simply the chief church in any particular parish, whether it be named Abbey, Priory, Minster, or simply Church.

Chapels

There are various types of chapel, as follows:

1. Part of a large church having a separate altar and dedicated differently from the main church. They are often known as side-chapels, and many are dedicated to the Blessed Virgin Mary and, in consequence, are called 'Lady' Chapels.

2. Chapels belonging to various institutions such as colleges, schools, prisons and hospitals. One of the most famous, architecturally, and for other reasons, is King's College Chapel, Cambridge.

3. 'Chapels of Ease' which are provided in some parishes for the use of worshippers living far away from the parish church.

4. Proprietary Chapels, of which there are now very few surviving, are those in private hands and usually part of some large private house.

5. Chapels Royal, which come under the direct jurisdiction of the Sovereign and are, therefore, not within the diocese of a bishop. They are served by priests directly appointed by the Crown under the 'Dean of the

Chapels Royal.' These Chapels are at St. James's Palace, Buckingham Palace, Windsor Castle, Sandringham, Hampton Court, Windsor Great Park, Balmoral, the Tower of London, the Queen's Chapel of the Savoy and the Chapel of St. Katharine, in Ratcliffe, near the Tower.

Church Dedications

As a rule churches are dedicated in honour of saints, a custom which arose certainly as early as the fourth century.

In England, in pre-Reformation times, the rite connected with the dedication of a church was divided into six principal parts: the blessing outside; the blessing in the middle of the church; the preparation for the consecration of the altar; the actual consecration of the altar; the procession of the relics; and the blessing of the altar vessels and ornaments. These were followed by a Mass.

In modern practice there is no set form, dioceses being left to arrange their own services, which are either a solemn consecration or a simple blessing. The former, which may be performed only by a bishop, is used for churches designed to be permanent, whereas the latter, which may be performed by a priest, is intended for a temporary structure.

The choice of the name of a new church rests with those responsible for having raised the money with which to build it, but it is usual to avoid repeating the name of an existing church in the same city, town or, should such a contingency arise, village.

The commonest dedications in England are: All Saints, St. Thomas, St. Andrew, St. Mary and St. Peter.

Churchyards and Cemeteries

A *churchyard* is the name given to the ground immediately surrounding a church, having definite boundaries, and the freehold of it is vested in the Rector, if there is one, or if not, then, usually, in the Vicar. The care and maintenance of a churchyard are among the duties of the Parochial Church Council.

It is the right of a resident in a parish to be buried in the parish churchyard, but the position of the grave is a matter for the incumbent to decide and it is not now, except in most unusual circumstances, possible for an individual to purchase a burial plot.

When a churchyard is full it can be legally declared a 'closed' churchyard, and the responsibility for its maintenance is handed over to the local authority. It can be converted to other use, such as a playground, without the removal of the remains of those who have been buried there.

A *cemetery* is the name given to a place, other than a churchyard, set apart for the burial of the dead, and its care and maintenance is among the duties of a district or parish council.

Church Interiors

Although there is an immense variety among the many thousands of churches in England, there are certain features common to them all. Thus in every church there is a chancel, or sanctuary, and a main central section, or nave.

The chancel, or sanctuary, is that part reserved for clergy and choir, while the nave, sometimes wrongly called the central aisle, is that part, between the main front and the chancel, which is assigned to the laity. When the far end of the chancel is semi-circular or polygonal it is called an 'apse.'

In addition to these features, there may be also one, or more, aisles, which are extensions of the nave made by piercing its side walls with arches, or there may be one or two transepts which are similar, but not so usual, extensions of the chancel. There may be, also, and there usually are in large churches, side chapels built out of the aisles.

In all churches there is a vestry which is a part of the church for the clergy and choir to vest in, and where various ornaments as well as registers are kept. This may be adapted from part of the original building or be a room added more recently.

Usually at the west end, or in the centre, there is a tower of some kind, but sometimes merely a bell-turret at the west end. Towers are found in the older churches and in the Middle Ages were often used as watch-towers. Spires and steeples arising out of towers are a later development.

As a rule, churches are built so that the chancel faces east, since the coming of the Lord was expected to be from that quarter. The main entrance, often with a porch, is usually on the south side, because in the main it is the 'best weather' side.

Sometimes there are cloisters added to the church and this is especially so in cases where there was formerly a monastic community. These are generally on the south side, although at Canterbury, Gloucester, Chester and Lincoln they are on the north. Cloisters are four-sided enclosures, often surrounded by covered ambulatories, and it was in them that the monks took exercise.

Inside the church are various objects, as follows:

Altar—a flat-topped block, or table, usually of wood, but occasionally of stone or marble, situated at the east end of the chancel, or sanctuary, and used for celebrating the Eucharist. Except on a very few occasions it is covered with a cloth, either multi-coloured, or of red, white, green, yellow or violet, according to the different seasons of the Church's year.

On the altar are placed a cross and either two or six candlesticks, containing candles. The significance of the cross is obvious, that of candles originated for the purpose of giving light but they have been retained as symbolic of Jesus, the 'Light of the World.' There may also be vases of flowers, a custom which began in the Western Church during the last century.

In many churches it is now usual to find flowers not on the altar itself but placed near it. During Lent, however, it is customary for flowers to be omitted altogether. Other objects used on an altar are a book containing the Eucharistic Service and, of course, during the Eucharist there are the Eucharistic vessels—namely the paten and the chalice, the former being the dish for containing the bread, the latter the cup containing the wine. During the Eucharist the top of the altar is covered with a white linen cloth, symbolical of the grave clothes of our Lord.

Reredos—sometimes there is some sort of decoration placed behind and above an altar. This is known as a reredos, and when there is no east window it may cover the entire east end wall. A *triptych* is a series of three panels set side by side. *Riddels* are side curtains set at right angles to the altar.

Altar rails—these were designed to protect the altar from profanation and were introduced into churches during the early part of Queen Elizabeth's reign. The Puritans removed them in many instances on the grounds that they implied a specially sacred aspect of the altar. In 1634 they were ordered to be restored, but seven years later Parliament again ordered their removal. In 1660 they were finally restored and have remained in most churches ever since. Used for communicants to kneel against as they receive the Sacrament they are generally of wood, but sometimes of wrought iron or brass, and have an entrance midway either in the form of a gate or by not being joined together there.

Credence table—a small table usually situated near to and to the south of the altar and used for holding the bread, wine and water for the Eucharist. The vessels containing the wine and water are called cruets.

Aumbry, or *Ambry*—a closed recess in the wall of a church in which the Sacrament is sometimes reserved.

Formerly it was used more for sacred vessels, relics and books.

Piscina—a basin formed by a niche in the wall on the south side of the altar and used for the priest to wash his hands after celebrating the Eucharist, and also for the washing of the chalice (the Ablutions). Occasionally two are to be found set side by side, one for the priest's hands, the other for the sacred vessels. Usually they have a shelf to hold the cruets and a drain connecting with the outside earth.

Sedilia—seats, usually three in number, i.e. for priest, deacon and sub-deacon, on the south side of the chancel. They are, as a rule, canopied and their use is for the priests to sit during certain parts of the Eucharist and other services when it is their custom to do so.

Sanctuary lamp—sometimes lamps are hung in front of an altar. There may be as many as seven, symbolical of the seven Gifts of the Holy Spirit. Also, it is usual in churches where the Sacrament is reserved for a white light to be hung before it.

Seats and reading desks—one, or possibly two, chairs, often carved, are generally to be found on either side of the altar. Primarily their use is for the Bishop or other visiting clergy. Choir stalls on either side of the chancel are also usual and a reading desk for the Incumbent.

So far the articles mentioned are those likely to be found within the chancel or Sanctuary. This part of the church may be divided from the nave by a *screen*, which when surmounted by a cross is known as a '*rood*' *screen*. They are usually of wood, often elaborately carved, but may also be of metal or stone, and date from the time when the chancel was the only part of the church and the congregation stood outside.

Between chancel and nave are the pulpit, lectern and Litany desk.

Pulpit—a raised stand for the preacher, made of wood or sometimes metal or stone and placed usually on the right or left side but sometimes in the middle of the nave according to which is the more convenient. Some date as far back as the fifteenth century. They are sometimes surmounted by a sounding-board. Sometimes pulpits are double or even three-deckers.

Lectern—a reading desk on a stand for holding liturgical books, and especially the Holy Bible. It is situated on the opposite side to the pulpit as a rule, but occasionally in the middle. It is made of wood or metal and is movable. Sometimes its form takes that of an eagle, symbol of St. John who gazed farther toward heaven than any other man (*Rev.* iv. 7). Less often it is that of a pelican, symbol of our Lord's redeeming work as mediated through the Blessed Sacrament, the pelican being depicted as drawing blood with her beak from her breast to feed her young.

Litany desk—a low movable desk from which in some churches it is customary for the Litany to be read.

Font—usually placed near the main entrance to the church at the west end of the nave as a symbol of the first step in Church membership. Made normally of stone, but occasionally of metal, and often octagonal in shape and carved. They are the receptacles for holding baptismal water. They are usually covered by a lid, sometimes a very elaborate one.

Other objects of interest in churches are:

Windows—often of stained glass depicting scriptural scenes, sometimes very old (twelfth century), sometimes very beautiful, and not seldom, unfortunately, garish and hideous. In modern churches plain glass is now more often used than stained with good results.

A 'Jesse' window is one which represents Christ's descent from Jesse, the father of David, usually taking the form of a tree. There is one in Wells Cathedral.

Hagioscope, or *Squint*—in some old churches there are openings in the chancel walls designed to enable worshippers in the side aisles, or the transepts, to see the altar during the elevation of the Host.

Organs—they date from as early as the eighth century and were in use in churches until 1644, when legislation for their destruction was ordered, but they were re-introduced in 1660. However, in many churches barrel organs or stringed instruments took their place until the nineteenth century when organs proper became general. In a few small country churches harmoniums are still the only musical instrument available.

Pews or other seating—originally no seating was provided for the congregation, except for stone seats attached to the walls and occasionally to the piers of the nave as a concession to the infirm. Hence the phrase 'the weakest go to the wall.' By the end of the thirteenth century many churches were, however, equipped also with a number of fixed wooden benches, which were often known as 'pews' (derived from the Latin *podium*, meaning a seat raised above floor level). These benches were often elaborately carved at the ends and back with grotesque animals, the heads of saints, and various other arrangements.

In a few churches chairs take the place of pews.

Roofs of the hammer-beam type are either single or double. The single consist of horizontal beams projecting from the walls about three feet, and vertical members on top of them supporting the rafters; the double consist of the same thing repeated again nearer the centre of the roof. Carved figures of angels, etc., occur.

Roofs of the collar-braced type, mainly fifteenth century, consist of a timber-pointed arch supporting the main rafters of the roof and like the hammer-beams occurs over the piers of the arcading, the intermediate rafters being supported by the wall plates, ridge-piece and purlins, these last being horizontal timbers running the length of the church at different intervals and heights according to the pitch of the rafters.[1]

Flags—The correct flag is that of St. George, either plain or with an escutcheon (in the first quarter) of the arms of the diocese in which the church is ecclesiastically

[1] *A Guide to English Architecture*, by C. J. W. Messent.

situated. This ruling was given in 1938 by the Earl Marshal.

Banners designed to be carried in processions are of various shapes, sizes, materials and colours.

Royal Arms—The display of royal arms in churches began at the time of the Reformation. Under Edward VI they sometimes replaced the rood (cross) in the chancel arch. Under Queen Mary I the roods were restored and the arms moved to some other place. During the Commonwealth they were mostly destroyed, but at the Restoration they were brought back. At the beginning of each reign they were changed, but the custom fell into disuse in Hanoverian times. They are to be found in various parts of the church often in the form of painted panels.

Sword Rests—These were usually of wrought iron, decorated and having the Royal or City or Mayoral Arms. They came into use after the Restoration, but very few of an earlier date than Queen Anne survive to-day.

Chests and Alms Boxes—The older ones of wood are often beautifully carved and have heavy hinges and padlocks. In more recent times metal safes are usually installed in the vestry.

Brasses—These are figures of a dead person engraved on a flat brass panel and let into the floor of a church. They date, as a rule, from the thirteenth to the sixteenth century, but many were taken out during the Reformation period.

Where church floors have had to be relaid, brasses have sometimes been taken up and fixed to an adjacent wall. Some are found with the reverse side also engraved, and these are known as 'palimpsest' brasses. They are of particular interest in giving information about contemporary dress, both lay and clerical.

Church Architecture

The various types of architecture are known as Anglo-Saxon, Norman, Gothic (Transitional, Early English,

Decorated, Perpendicular), Renaissance, Georgian, Gothic Revival and Twentieth Century.

In many instances churches contain an amalgamation of various styles, particularly the older buildings in which alterations have taken place at various times throughout the centuries.

For those interested in details recourse to an architectural handbook is advisable.

Church Registers

In each parish, registers of baptisms, banns of marriages and burials, as well as the parish duplicate of the marriage register, are kept. These belong to the parish, and their custodian is the incumbent of the parish, or, in the event of a vacancy in the benefice, the churchwardens.

For those desiring to have registers 'searched' there is a statutory fee payable.

CHAPTER SIX

MISCELLANEOUS

Yew Trees in Churchyards

The prevalence of yew trees in country churchyards is probably due to their longevity, many attaining an age of several hundred years and therefore not needing to be soon replaced and so symbolizing lasting life. On the other hand some theorists declare that they were planted in obedience to royal decrees in order to provide wood for long-bows and that churchyards were chosen as being unlikely places for cattle and sheep to stray in, the yew being injurious to such animals if eaten by them.

Hot Cross Buns

The custom of eating hot cross buns on Good Friday is derived from a pagan habit, common to both Greeks and Romans, of eating bread marked with a cross at public sacrifices, such bread being usually purchased at the doors of the temple and taken inside to be eaten. Incidentally, the term 'Good Friday,' which may seem inappropriate for this particular day, is probably a corruption of 'God's Friday.'

Rushbearing

Although the ancient custom of annually renewing the rushes which covered the floors of many churches has long ceased, it is still commemorated in a few parishes in England, of which the best known is Ambleside in Westmorland where each year, on the Saturday nearest to St. Anne's Day (July 26th), there is a procession of children carrying floral crowns through the streets before offering them in the church. The procession halts in the market-place where the rushbearing hymn is sung. The vicar, verger, churchwardens, etc., also march.

Inside the church can now be seen a mural, twenty-six feet long by twelve feet high, depicting the ceremony. It was painted by a young artist who was stationed at Ambleside during the Second World War and dedicated by the Bishop of Carlisle in July, 1944.

Curiously, of the few parishes where rushbearing still takes place, two others are the adjoining parishes of Warcop and Musgrave, also in Westmorland.

Candlemas

The feast commemorating the Purification of the Blessed Virgin Mary and the presentation of Christ in the temple is celebrated on February 2nd. The blessing of the candles which is the distinctive rite of this feast probably did not come into use until the eleventh century. If there is a procession those taking part in it do so holding lighted candles. The symbolism is that of the 'light of the world' being brought into the temple.

Maundy Money

The money distributed on Maundy Thursday by the Sovereign to a certain number of poor men and women in Westminster Abbey takes the place of the ancient custom of washing the feet of paupers by highly-placed persons such as bishops in their cathedrals and abbots in their monasteries.

Shrove Tuesday

The day before Ash Wednesday is so called from the 'shriving' (i.e. confession and absolution) as a preliminary to the season of Lent.

It is sometimes called 'Pancake Tuesday,' the eating of pancakes on this day being a survival of the times when it was the last day of feasting and merry-making prior to the long Lenten fast.

Several odd happenings are associated with the day. One of these was the 'thrashing of the hen,' a cruel custom consisting of blind-fold boys armed with branches of trees who endeavoured to land their blows on a wretched hen securely attached to the back of another boy. After the poor bird had been finally put out of her misery she was boiled with bacon and eaten along with the pancakes! Another custom, particularly prevalent in the north of England, was cock-fighting in the schools, for which each boy presented a 'cock-penny' to the headmaster.

It need hardly be added that there is no religious significance attached to these events!

Academical Hoods

The academic hoods likely to be seen as part of the dress of a clergyman are:

D.D.—Oxford: Scarlet cloth (C.S.),[1] lined with black silk.

Cambridge: Scarlet cloth (C.S.), lined with pink silk.

Durham: Scarlet cassimere (C.S.), lined with palatinate purple silk.

London: Scarlet cassimere (C.S.), lined with Sarum red silk.

B.D.—Oxford, Cambridge, Durham: Black silk (C.S.), lined with the same.

London: Black silk or staff (C.S.), edged on inside with Sarum red silk (but with white silk for members of Convocations).

M.A.—Oxford: Black silk, lined with crimson silk (O.S.).[2]

Cambridge: Black silk, lined with white silk (C.S.).

Durham: Black silk, lined with palatinate purple silk (O.S.).

[1] C.S.—Hood and tippet. [2] O.S.—Oxford Shape, the cowl alone.

London: Black silk, lined with russet brown silk (C.S.).

B.A. —Oxford: Black stuff, edged with white fur (O.S.).

Cambridge: Black stuff, edged with white fur (C.S.).

Durham: Black stuff, edged with white fur (C.S.).

London: Black silk, or stuff, edged with russet brown (C.S.).

Lampeter: Black silk, or stuff, edged on inside and bound with miniver (C.S.).

There are many others.

Grace at Meals

Although not exclusively Christian, the custom of giving thanks both before and after meals seems a very natural one for a Christian to adopt, and it has been in use in Christian households since the earliest days of the Church. It takes many forms. One of the more frequently used is: 'For what we are about to receive, may the Lord make us truly thankful,' followed by, 'For what we have received may the Lord make us truly thankful.' Others are in Latin, while in certain schools, colleges and other communal establishments it is not unusual to find a fixed and often lengthy form attached to a board and read by an official. Saying 'Grace' has greatly declined in recent years, although when a clergyman is present at a meal it is still quite customary for the host or hostess to ask him to do so.

Family Prayers

Like the saying of Grace at meals, family prayers are very much a thing of the past. They were started after the Reformation, and spread in Elizabethan times. Even so late as 1889 the then Provost of King's College, Cambridge, in a circular letter addressed to the undergraduates of the college, wrote, '. . . You, most of you, come from homes where family prayers are the custom.' One doubts whether that remark would apply to the undergraduates of King's, or any other college, to-day!

It was during the last years of Queen Victoria's reign that the custom began to lapse.

Oxford Movement

The Oxford, or Tractarian, Movement was initiated in 1833 by John Keble's sermon on national apostasy, preached before the Judges of Assize at Oxford in July of that year. There followed the first of the 'Tracts for the Times' written by various men, including Newman, Froude and Pusey, who shared Keble's views.

The Movement was designed as a defence of the Church of England as a Divine institution and of the doctrine of the Apostolic Succession. It was a 'high-church' protest against the 'low-church,' an insistence on English Catholicism in reaction to the Evangelical revival. It may be said to have ended in 1845, when Newman and others in the Movement were received into the Church of Rome, but its influence was considerable and has lasted.

The Oxford Movement has no connection whatsoever with the *Oxford Group*, the name given, for some extraordinary reason, to a movement, founded in 1938 by a Lutheran American of Swiss descent, Frank Buchman (*b.* 1878), but more properly called Buchmanism or Moral Re-armament (M.R.A.).

Canon Law

Canon law is defined as the body of ecclesiastical rules or laws imposed by authority in matters of faith, morals and discipline. (The word Canon comes from the Greek word *Kanon*, meaning a rule of conduct.)

These 'canons' were made from time to time by various Councils and Synods and collections of them began to be made in the fourth century.

In 1604 a body of 141 canons was passed by the Canterbury Convocation and by the York Convocation two years later. They received the royal assent and survive, with only a few amendments and modifications, as the canon law of the Church to-day. But their revision, which began in 1939 when a Commission was appointed by the Archbishops of Canterbury and York for the purpose, is still in progress. In 1947 the Commission issued a report, 'The Canon Law of the Church of England,' which included a collection of draft canons arranged under the following headings:

1. The Church of England.
2. Divine Service and Administration of the Sacraments.
3. Ministers, their Ordination, Functions and Charge.
4. The Order of Deaconesses.
5. The Lay Officers of the Church of England.
6. Things Appertaining to Churches.
7. The Ecclesiastical Courts.
8. The Synods, Assemblies and Conferences of the Church of England.

Church Army

It was founded in 1882 by the late Prebendary Wilson Carlile, C.H., D.D., and consists of a body of laymen and women. Its activities include social and moral welfare among the poor, overseas mission work, hostels for women and girls, work among H.M. Forces both at home and abroad, whole-time service in prisons, etc. It is pledged to the doctrine and practice of the Church of England and its officers work under the bishops and clergy. The men are known as 'Captains' and the women as 'Sisters' and they have a training college in London. Their uniform is grey-coloured service style. They are essentially evangelists.

Church of England Children's Society

Formerly known as the 'Waifs and Strays Society' this is a society formed for rescuing and caring for children in need, especially babies and very small children. At present the society cares for between four and five thousand children, and seventy-four thousand have been provided for since it was formed in 1881. It has various homes and religious training is undertaken by local parochial clergy. It is neither nationalized nor state subsidized and so has to rely on voluntary contributions for its funds. It is a registered adoption society.

Octave

The name given to the eighth day after a particular church festival, the feast day itself and the 'octave' being counted, so that it falls always on the same day of the week as the feast itself. Any event occurring during the period is said to be 'within the octave' and some commemoration of the feast in question is observed throughout the period.

Cantor and Cantoris

A cantor is a singer who pre-intones and leads in the liturgical music of the choir, and 'Cantoris' is the name given to the north side of the choir. The opposite side is known as 'Decani' (the south side of a Cathedral which is where the Dean normally has his stall).

Defender of the Faith

A title first bestowed (1521) on King Henry VIII by Pope Leo X and recognized by Parliament (1544) as an official title of the monarch. It has since been borne by every English Sovereign.

Faculty

A licence granted by the Judge of an Ecclesiatical Court to authorize alterations or additions to the fabric, fittings or ornaments of a church.

Missionary Work of the Church

It has often been stated that the primary duty of the Church lies in evangelization and, indeed, the propagation of the Christian faith among non-Christian people has been one of its main tasks from earliest times and has continued ever since.

To-day there are very many missionary societies, the chief of which are the Society for the Propagation of the Gospel in Foreign Parts (S.P.G.), the Church Missionary Society (C.M.S.), the Society for Promoting Christian Knowledge (S.P.C.K.), the Universities' Mission to Central Africa (U.M.C.A.), the Bible Churchmen's Missionary Society (B.C.M.S.) and the British and Foreign Bible Society.

There is also the 'Conference of Missionary Societies in Great Britain and Ireland,' which was formed in 1912 and embraces sixty British Missionary Societies, including those referred to above.

'High' and 'Low' Church

These terms are freely used to differentiate between two types of Churchmanship: Anglo-Catholic and Evangelical.

Thus, 'high' churchmen stress the continuity of the Church of England with Catholic Christianity, the claims of the episcopate and the priesthood, and the saving grace of Sacraments. Whereas 'low' churchmen approximate more to protestant non-conformity and give a low place to the authority of bishops and priests, the inherent grace of Sacraments, and ritual. The term 'high' as applied to churchmen dates back to the end of the seventeenth century, and that of 'low' was later coined in contrast to them, and they have continued ever since, becoming especially marked at the time of the Oxford Movement.

Another 'term,' now fallen into disuse, was 'Broad' and this referred to those who objected to positive definition in theology and sought to interpret the Anglican formularies and rubrics in a broad and liberal sense. Their successors are now generally known as Modernists.

A colloquial word for High Churchmen is 'spiky,' indicating those who possess hard, unyielding views!

The inherent inconsistency which is one of the characteristics of 'human nature' renders the terms 'high' and 'low' comparative and in practice there are varying degrees of both. In any case, they share fundamental beliefs and are committed to the Creeds, the Lord's Prayer, the Ten Commandments and the Book of Common Prayer.

Crucifixes

Up to the time of the Reformation crucifixes were common in churches, especially in the centre of the Rood Screen, but after the Reformation it was very unusual indeed for them to be seen, although they were very occasionally used on the altar. Nor was it until the nineteenth century and the Oxford Movement that they again appeared at all frequently, and even to-day there are certainly many more churches not containing one than the reverse.

A very usual place to find a crucifix in those churches which contain them is by the side of the pulpit. 'I preach Jesus Christ and Him crucified' (St. Paul).

The Mothers' Union

The Mothers' Union was started by Mrs. Sumner (née Heywood) at Old Alresford, in Hampshire, in order to demonstrate 'the ideals of a holy and unbreakable marriage, of Christian education for the children, and of personal witness by each individual woman to her Lord and Master.'[1]

For a time it existed only in Alresford and a few neighbouring parishes, but after Mrs. Sumner's husband

[1] *A Short Memoir of Mary Sumner*, by J. Vaughan.

had become Archdeacon of Winchester, in 1885, it was soon established as a Winchester Diocesan Society, and when, in 1888, the Archdeacon became Suffragan Bishop of Guildford it began to spread considerably. In 1926 it was incorporated by Royal Charter and it is very much alive to-day. Incidentally, there appears to be no need to be a mother to be a member!

The Sign of the Cross

The signification of this is the dedication to Christ of what is about to be done or what has been done. It is the sign used in Baptism, Confirmation, and other rites of the Church.

It is made by drawing the right hand from forehead to breast and then from shoulder to shoulder, left to right, 'In the Name of the Father, the Son, and the Holy Ghost. Amen.'

Methodism

The movement, to which the name of Methodism was given, arose within the Church of England as a mission movement, and it is interesting to note that its three founders—the 'High Church' brothers Charles and John Wesley, and the 'Calvinistic' George Whitefield—were all three of them priests. It arose as a reaction against the apathy of the Church at the time (early part of the eighteenth century), and it is one of the tragedies in the history of the Church that although John Wesley (the effective founder) lived and died a priest of the Church of England ('the purest in Christendom,' he said), his followers cut themselves off from the Mother-church shortly after his death.

However, in more recent times, the degree of disagreement has been to some extent decreased, and discussions between the Church of England and the Methodist Church have been held to explore the prospect of reconciliation.

Crockford's Clerical Directory

This book of reference for facts relating to the Clergy and the Church of England was first published in 1857. It is issued biennially and is to be found in most public libraries. Among other things it gives details of the careers of members of the Anglican ministry.

The Official Year Book of the Church of England

This is an annual publication issued by the Church Information Office of the Church Assembly and is a mine of information concerning the work of the Church both at home and overseas.

The Church Times

A weekly newspaper founded at the height of the Anglo-Catholic revival in 1863. Published every Friday, price 5*d.*

The Church of England Newspaper

A weekly newspaper, published every Friday, price 6*d.*

Church Illustrated

A monthly magazine, price 6*d.*, illustrated.

Note: Most parishes print a parish magazine, and many dioceses a diocesan magazine.

The Seven Sacraments

(1) Baptism, (2) Confirmation, (3) The Eucharist, (4) Penance, (5) Extreme Unction, (6) Orders, and (7) Matrimony are the traditional Seven Sacraments.

In the Church of England the Sacraments are divided thus:

The two greater Sacraments: (1) Baptism, (2) Holy Communion.

The five lesser Sacraments: (1) Confirmation, (2) Confession and Absolution, (3) Ordination, (4) Unction, (5) Marriage.

The Seven Deadly Sins

(1) Pride, (2) Anger, (3) Gluttony, (4) Lust, (5) Covetousness, (6) Envy, (7) Sloth.

The sin against the Holy Ghost, the unforgivable sin (of St. Matthew and St. Luke), is sometimes described as the sin of declaring good to be evil, knowing that it is not so.

The Seven Gifts of the Holy Ghost

(1) Wisdom, (2) Understanding, (3) Counsel, (4) Fortitude, (5) Knowledge, (6) Piety, (7) Fear of the Lord (*Isa.* xi. 2).

Holy Ghost and Holy Spirit

Some confusion of mind may arise from the fact that both these terms are used to describe the Third Person of the Holy Trinity. There is, however, no difference between them except for the wording.

Various Emblems

Holy Spirit—Dove.
St. Matthew—A winged man; a carpenter's square.
St. Mark—A winged lion.
St. Luke—A winged ox, or calf.
St. John—An eagle; a cup with snake or dragon emerging from it.
St. Peter—Two keys.
St. Paul—A sword and a closed book.
St. Andrew—A cross—X.
St. James the Great—A pilgrim's hat, staff, wallet and scallop shell.
St. Philip—A tall cross; basket containing loaves of bread.
St. Bartholomew—A flaying knife.
St. James the Less—A club.

St. Simon—A saw; a fish.
St. Jude—A halberd; holding a boat.
St. Matthias—A spear; an axe.
St. Thomas—A carpenter's rule; a spear.
St. Michael—A sword, standing over, or fighting with a dragon.
St. John the Baptist—A lamb.
St. George—A dragon.
Martyrs in general—A palm and a crown.
Saints in general—A nimbus, or circular halo, round the head.

Abbreviations

A. & M. — Hymns Ancient and Modern.
A.K.C. — Associate of King's College.
A.L.C.D. — Associate of the London College of Divinity.
A.M.D.G. — To the Greater Glory of God (Ad majorem Dei gloriam).
A.V. — Authorized Version.
B.C.P. — Book of Common Prayer.
B.D. — Bachelor of Divinity.
B.V.M. — Blessed Virgin Mary.
C. of E. — Church of England.
C.E.M.S. — Church of England Men's Society.
C.F. — Chaplain to the Forces.
C.M.S. — Church Missionary Society.
C.U. — Church Union (formerly—'English Church Union').
D.C.T. — Doctor of Christian Theology.
D.D. — Doctor of Divinity.
D.Th. — Doctor of Theology.
D.G. — By the Grace of God (Dei gratia).
F.R.C.O. — Fellow of the Royal College of Organists.
H.C.F. — Honorary Chaplain to the Forces.
I.H.S. — Jesus the Saviour of Mankind (Iesus Hominum Salvator). Also the first three letters of the Greek form of Jesus.
I.N.R.I. — Jesus of Nazareth, King of the Jews (Iesus Nazarenus Rex Iudaeorum).
L.Div. — Licentiate in Divinity.
M.Th. — Master of Theology.
N.T. — New Testament.

O.S.B.	—	Order of St. Benedict.
O.T.	—	Old Testament.
Q.H.C.	—	Honorary Chaplain to the Queen.
R.D.	—	Rural Dean.
R.T.S.	—	Religious Tract Society.
Rt. Rev.	—	Right Reverend (Bishop).
R.V.	—	Revised Version.
S.P.C.K.	—	Society for the Promotion of Christian Knowledge.
S.P.G.	—	Society for the Propagation of the Gospel.
S.S.F.	—	Franciscan Order.
Y.M.C.A.	—	Young Men's Christian Association.
Y.W.C.A.	—	Young Women's Christian Association.

Religious Communities

Men

The Community of the Resurrection, Mirfield, Yorks.
Society of St. John the Evangelist, Oxford.
Society of the Sacred Mission, Kelham, Notts.
Order of St. Benedict, Nashdom Abbey, Burnham, Bucks.
The Society of St. Francis, Cerne Abbas, Dorset.
The Brotherhood of the Holy Cross, Linden Grove, Peckham.
Oratory of the Good Shepherd, Cambridge.
Order of St. Paul, Alton, Hants.
The Society of the Holy Cross, Peterborough, Northants.

Women

The Community of the Holy Rood, Middlesbrough, Yorks.
Order of the Holy Paraclete, Whitby, Yorks.
The Sisters of Bethany, Lloyd Square, London, W.C.1.
St. Saviour's Priory, Queensbridge Road, London, E.2.
St. Mary's Convent, Burlington Lane, Chiswick, W.4.
Sisters of the Church, Ham Common, Surrey.
Community of St. Francis, 155 Richmond Road, Hackney, E.8.
Order of St. Mary at the Cross, Edgware.

Order of St. Elizabeth of Hungary, 94 Redcliffe Gardens, London, S.W.10.

Canonesses Regular of Our Lady of Victory, Hale Lane, Edgware.

Sisters of St. Peter the Apostle, Staines, Middlesex.

Community of the Presentation, 6 North Hill, Highgate, N.6.

Deaconess Community of St. Andrew, 12 Tavistock Crescent, London, W.11.

Society of the Hidden Life, Lloyd Square, London, W.C.1.

Society of Incarnation, Birmingham.

The Sisters of Charity, Bristol.

Community of the Sacred Passion, Chelmsford, Essex.

Community of the Blessed Virgin Mary, Rottingdean, Sussex.

Community of the Holy Cross, Haywards Heath, Sussex.

Community of the Holy Family, St. Leonard's-on-Sea, Sussex.

Society of St. Margaret, East Grinstead, Sussex.

Confraternity of the Divine Love, Heathfield, Sussex.

Community of the Nursing Sisters of St. John the Divine, Hastings, Sussex.

Community of St. Lawrence, Belper, Derbyshire.

Community of St. Wilfrid, Exeter.

Community of the Companions of Jesus the Good Shepherd, Newton Abbot, S. Devon.

The Franciscan Servants of Jesus and Mary, Crediton, Devon.

Community of Jesus of Nazareth, Kingham, Oxford.

Community of the Compassion of Jesus, Thames Ditton, Surrey.

St. Peter's Convent, Woking, Surrey.

Sisterhood of All Hallows, Ditchingham, Norfolk.

Community of St. John the Baptist, Clewer, Berks.

Community of St. Mary the Virgin, Wantage, Berks.

Society of the Holy and Undivided Trinity, Malvern Link, Worcs.

St. Thomas's Convent, Oxford.

Society of the Holy Trinity, Ascot, Berks.
Society of the Precious Blood, Maidenhead, Berks.
Community of the Sisters of the Love of God, Oxford.
Servants of Christ, Burnham, Bucks.
Society of the Good Shepherd, Twyford, Berks.
Order of St. Anne, Emsworth, Hants.
Benedictine Community, West Malling, Kent.
Community of All Saints, St. Albans, Herts.
Community of St. Denys, Warminster, Wilts.
Community of Reparation to Jesus in the Blessed Sacrament, Woking, Surrey.
Community of the Epiphany, Truro, Cornwall.
Community of St. Peter, Horbury, Yorks.
Community of the Holy Name, Malvern Link, Worcs.

From this list it will be seen that there are nine monastic, or religious, orders for men and forty-eight for women. Mostly these communities are engaged in pastoral, evangelistic, educational and literary activities either at home or abroad. Many conduct retreats. A few are 'enclosed,' in which the members devote themselves largely to contemplative prayer.

Their work, though little publicized or advertised, is essentially of great spiritual influence. In order to become a member of such a community the usual course is to spend a period in the Community house as a guest. The next step is to become a Novice and afterwards, if considered suitable by the Superior, to take life vows.

In the above list only the address of the main Community Centre has been given, but many of the orders have numerous other houses. Mowbrays' *Guide to the Religious Communities of the Anglican Communion* gives details of these.

The Church and Divorce

There are few matters connected with the Church which give rise to more controversy than its attitude to the question of divorce and the re-marriage of divorced persons, and yet its position with regard to them is surely quite clear.

The Church bases its doctrine of marriage on the teaching of Jesus Christ and regards it as a union which is indissoluble save by the death of one of the parties.

A divorce is therefore a dissolution by the State of a marriage which in the opinion of the Church is indissoluble, and it can hardly be expected that the Church should consider that what the State allows is to supersede what in its opinion is the teaching of Christ.

As to how the teaching of Christ on this question should be interpreted may, and does, vary with different individuals but remains constant in the case of the Church. It is based on passages in St. Mark's and in St. Matthew's Gospels, where Christ is recorded as saying:

'For this cause shall a man leave his father and mother, and cleave to his wife; and they twain shall be one flesh: so then they are no more twain, but one flesh. What therefore God hath joined together, let not man put asunder' (*St. Mark* x. 7–9), and in St. Luke's Gospel:

'Whosoever putteth away his wife, and marrieth another, committeth adultery: and whosoever marrieth her that is put away from her husband committeth adultery' (*St. Luke* xvi. 18).

It seems often to be forgotten that the Church cannot but assume that those who ask it to solemnize their marriage do so in acceptance of its teaching on the subject. Those who do not accept it can be legally married by a civil registrar.

To ask the Church to solemnize a marriage in which both parties promise to keep to each other 'till death do us part' and then to expect the same Church to condone their divorce is surely to make a mockery of Church and marriage service.

The Church, however, does in certain cases recognize judicial separation, but in such cases the parties cannot re-marry.

In the event of a marriage being not consummated it is

possible for a decree of nullity to be granted by the Courts and in this event the Church holds that both parties may re-marry, the former marriage being regarded as 'no marriage.'

No clergyman can be compelled to marry any person whose former marriage has been dissolved on any ground and whose former partner is still living, or to permit such a marriage in his church.

With regard to the right of admission to Holy Communion of divorced people the Church holds that there is no objection to those who do not re-marry during the lifetime of the former spouse, but this does not apply to those who do so re-marry, although the exclusion is not necessarily perpetual. That is for the Bishop to decide.

The Books of Homilies

There were two books of Homilies appointed to be read in the churches, the first being published in 1547 and the second in 1574, 'for stay of such errors as were then by ignorant preachers sparkled among the people.'

In Article XXXV of the Thirty-nine Articles both these books are referred to as containing 'a godly and wholesome Doctrine' and the names of the Homilies are listed. They were composed by different authors, among whom was Thomas Cranmer, and were freely used by the less learned of the clergy in place of sermons.

Their object was to provide the clergy with subjects suitable for discourse during a period of transition and so to prevent them, or some of them, from preaching about certain points of doctrine which were liable to cause trouble!

Apostle

By 'apostle' is indicated the chief disciples of Jesus Christ. These were Andrew, Bartholomew, James (son of Zebedee), James (son of Alphaeus), John, Judas (son of James), Judas Iscariot, Matthew, Nathanael, Peter, Philip, Simon, Thaddeus and Thomas.

The term is also applied to Matthias, Paul and Barnabas.

Disciple

The word is used alternatively to describe the apostles, but also means any of the earlier followers of Christ and, indeed, any follower since.

Evangelist

The four authors of the canonical Gospels, i.e. Matthew, Mark, Luke and John, are so described.

The word is also used of particular preachers of the Gospel and those doing missionary work.

Martyr

The name given to those who have suffered death for the Christian faith.

The Stations of the Cross

In some churches a series of fourteen pictures or carvings are to be seen ranged round the walls and depicting various incidents in Christ's journey from the house of Pontius Pilate to the entombment. They are known as the Stations of the Cross, and commemorate the following events: (1) the condemnation by Pilate, (2) the reception of the Cross, (3) His first fall, (4) the meeting with His mother, (5) Simon of Cyrene carrying the Cross, (6) Veronica wiping Christ's face, (7) His second fall, (8) the exhortation to the women of Jerusalem, (9) His third fall, (10) the stripping of the clothes, (11) the Crucifixion, (12) His death on the Cross, (13) the descent from the Cross, (14) the burial in the tomb.

During Lent and Passiontide the Stations are visited in turn, prayers are recited, and those taking part meditate for a while on each incident.

The Seven Words from the Cross

On Good Friday it is customary in many churches for a special service, called the Three Hours' Devotion, to be held, at which, more often than not, the Seven Words from the Cross are used as texts. These are: (1) 'Father, forgive them; for they know not what they do' (*St. Luke* xxiii. 34); (2) 'To-day shalt thou be with Me in Paradise' (*St. Luke* xxiii. 43); (3) 'Woman, behold thy son . . . Behold thy mother' (*St. John* xix. 26f.); (4) 'Eli, Eli, lama sabachthani?' [that is to say] 'My God, My God, why hast Thou forsaken Me?' (*St. Matt.* xxvii. 46; *St. Mark* xv. 34); (5) 'I thirst' (*St. John* xix. 28); (6) 'It is finished' (*St. John* xix. 30); (7) 'Father, into Thy hands I commend My spirit' (*St. Luke* xxiii. 46).

Santa Claus

These two familiar words are a corruption of the Dutch form of Saint Nicholas, who is widely venerated as the patron of children. It was the Dutch Protestants in New Amsterdam, America, who started the custom of making Christmas presents in his name, and the custom spread to England. His feast day is December 6th. The prevalent habit of referring to him as just 'Santa' is, of course, quite meaningless.

Alleluia!

This word, which occurs in several of the Psalms, in two other places in the Holy Bible, and in many hymns is an expression of praise to God and is derived from the Hebrew word meaning 'Praise ye Yah.'

The Cardinal Virtues are justice, prudence, temperance and fortitude.

The Theological Virtues are faith, hope and charity.

The Oecumenical Movement

The interest on the part of the Church of England in this movement, developed to recover a basic unity of all Christian believers transcending creed, ritual and organization, dates from the Edinburgh Missionary Conference of 1910.

Although some progress towards achieving this object has been made it cannot be said that there is yet anything approaching real unity. But the World Council of Churches, which first met in 1948, and is world-wide, has to some extent brought together most of the Churches (with the exception of the Church of Rome) which acknowledge Jesus Christ as Saviour and God, and the International Missionary Council with which it is closely associated has helped towards this end.

The functions of the World Council of Churches are defined in its Constitution as follows:

1. To carry on the work of the two world movements for Faith and Order and for Life and Work.
2. To facilitate common action by the Churches.
3. To promote co-operation in study.
4. To promote the growth of oecumenical consciousness in the members of all Churches.
5. To establish relations with denominational federations of world-wide scope and with other oecumenical movements.
6. To call World Conferences on specific subjects as occasion may require, such conferences being empowered to publish their own findings.

Books Consulted and Recommended for Reference and Further Reading

The Oxford Dictionary of the Christian Church, edited by F. L. Cross. O.U.P., 1957.

The Church of England in the Twentieth Century (2 vols.), by Roger Lloyd. Longmans Green & Co., 1946 and 1950.

The Church of England, by Guy Mayfield. O.U.P., 1958.

In an Age of Revolution, by Cyril Garbett. Hodder & Stoughton, 1952.

The English Inheritance, by G. Kitson Clark. S.C.M. Press, Ltd., 1950.

The Parson's Handbook, by Percy Dearmer. Grant Richards, 1899.

The Official Year Book of the Church of England. S.P.C.K., 1958.

Doctrine in the Church of England. S.P.C.K., 1938.

The Church of England, by H. Hensley Henson. C.U.P., 1939.

English Social History, by G. M. Trevelyan. Longmans Green & Co., 1942.

A Guide to English Architecture, by C. J. W. Messent.

Exploring English Character, by Geoffrey Gorer. Cresset Press, 1955.

Church and People, 1789–1889, by S. C. Carpenter, B.D. S.P.C.K., 1933.

The English Country Parson, by William Addison. J. M. Dent & Sons, 1947.

Randall Davidson, by G. K. A. Bell. O.U.P., 1952.

William Temple, by F. A. Iremonger. O.U.P., 1948.

Cosmo Gordon Lang, by J. G. Lockhart. Hodder & Stoughton, 1949.

Retrospect of an Unimportant Life, by H. Hensley Henson. O.U.P. (1942–1950).

Query Corner, arranged by A. J. Bryant, M.B.E. A. R. Mowbray & Co. (1957).

INDEX